TELEVISION
AND
AGGRESSION

An Experimental
Field Study

Seymour Feshbach
and
Robert D. Singer

TELEVISION AND AGGRESSION

Jossey-Bass Inc., Publishers
San Francisco • London • Washington • 1977

TELEVISION AND AGGRESSION
An Experimental Field Study
Seymour Feshbach and Robert D. Singer

Library of Congress Catalog Card Number 70-138457

International Standard Book Number ISBN 0-87589-083-0

Manufactured in the United States of America

JACKET DESIGN BY WILLI BAUM

FIRST EDITION
First printing: December 1970
Second printing: February 1977

Code 7034

The Jossey-Bass
Behavioral Science Series

Preface

Television and Aggression arises from a study which is addressed to an important contemporary social issue—the effects of the portrayal of violence in television upon the preadolescent and adolescent boys who are among the principal viewers of such programs. A serious concern exists among the public and among professional social scientists that such content serves as a model for impressionable youth, fostering aggressive thoughts and actions which may sometimes take an antisocial form. The depiction of violence, it is felt, may act as a go-ahead signal, stimulating aggressive impulses and reducing the inhibitions which the culture has inculcated against the commission of aggressive acts. Thus television, with its mass audience and its omnipresence in the American family's living room, is seen by some as a possible contributing

factor to the prevalence of street and campus riots, delinquent acts
entailing injury to people and property, and other forms of violence
during the past decade.

A differing view, held by some social scientists, psychiatrists,
artists, and members of the communication industry, does not deny
the possibility that violence in television may arouse tendencies to
aggression in some children but argues that other possible effects
of television should be considered in evaluating its potential impact.
Among these effects are entertainment, which may relax tensions
and distract the viewer from the real world of conflict and violence,
and the catharsis of hostile feelings, which could result if the dramatic presentation of violence on television provided aggressive
children an opportunity to work through their hostile impulses
vicariously in socially acceptable fantasies. A third position in es-
sence states that exposure to violence on television is irrelevant to
the occurrence of aggression in the real world.

The verdict of research on these issues is ambiguous. Clear-
cut answers are difficult to provide because the issue is not simply
whether violence in television stimulates, reduces, or has no effect
upon children's aggression. Many variables may have a critical
bearing upon the effects of exposure to aggression on television.
These variables include the type and degree of violence depicted;
the overall dramatic context; the outcome of the violence; the personal attractiveness of the aggressor; the justifiability of the aggressive acts depicted; the degree of prior exposure; the age, intelligence,
aggressive predisposition, emotional state, and stability of the audience; and the nature of the viewer's aggressive reaction. And this
list is by no means exhaustive.

One of the problems in drawing inferences from laboratory
experiments on the effects of aggression in television is the large
number of determining variables involved in the natural viewing
context. Although the laboratory studies can help illuminate some
of these variables and the psychological processes involved, field
studies directly evaluating the TV viewing behavior of children and
their subsequent reactions are very much needed. However, a major
drawback to most field studies is the inability to provide the degree
of experimental control that can be achieved in a laboratory experi-

ment. The study reported in *Television and Aggression* was an effort to employ laboratory procedures in a field context.

Through the cooperation of a number of private schools and boys' homes controls were instituted over the television viewing behavior of preadolescent and adolescent boys so that they were systematically exposed to television programs which were either predominantly aggressive or predominantly nonaggressive in content. These controls were exercised for a six-week period. In addition to assessing changes in aggressive attitudes and values resulting from the differential television exposure, we also obtained indices of the number and type of aggressive acts in which each child engaged during the experimental exposure period. Some difficulties were encountered in implementing an experiment of this scope, but we were able to enlist the interest of the boys and maintain the variation in television exposure for the designated six weeks. The efforts to obtain measures of the boys' aggressive attitudes and actions also met with a reasonably high degree of success. No experiment in the area of human behavior is perfect, however. In undertaking this study we were aware of some of its methodological limitations, and we attempted to compensate for them or to statistically evaluate their effects where possible.

In spite of imperfections, we believe that the results of the study have an important bearing on the current controversy over the portrayal of aggressive events on television. Although we had predicted that a significant subgroup of participants would become more aggressive as a result of exposure to the aggressive TV diet, we did not find this change to occur. If there were stimulating effects they were too weak to be detected in overt behavior or attitudes by our procedures, and, we suggest, unlikely to be of much practical or social importance. Moreover, we found consistent evidence in particular and identifiable groups of reduced aggression as a result of exposure to the aggressive television diet. The latter effect was partly unanticipated, and before prescribing exposure to aggressive television as a therapeutic measure we would want further empirical support of these results.

We feel reasonably confident, however, that the violent program content which these boys observed is not a significant cause of their aggression. This statement has important limitations. It is not meant to be a license for the realistic portrayal of bloody, sadistic, overly violent actions. While this type of violence can be observed in motion pictures, it is not characteristic of the kind of aggressive events typically depicted on television. We would permit our own children to watch the violence presented on television, but we would not permit them to be exposed to the violence depicted in some contemporary motion pictures. There are other restrictions as well. We did not study girls or children of nursery or early elementary school age. Younger children may well have very different reactions to aggressive television content than do children in the age range of our sample. Furthermore, these results cannot be generalized to children raised in other cultures.

In any case, the findings indicate that we must be discriminating in our evaluation of the effects of the portrayal of violence on television. Blanket indictments of aggressive content, regardless of the dramatic context or the character of the audience, are inappropriate. Violence in the guise of dramatic fantasy is found throughout history and it seems likely that the vicarious participation in these fantasies does satisfy some human needs.

This research project could not have been carried out without the assistance and cooperation of a number of individuals and organizations. The responsibility for the research design, its implementation, and the statements in this report is ours. However, we wish to acknowledge the many contributions made by others to this project.

A major debt of gratitude is owed the staffs of Cate School, McKinley Home, Pacific Lodge Home, Army and Navy Academy, Ojai Valley School, St. Vincent's Home, and St. John's Home. The experimental program was a significant intrusion on each institution and created extra burdens for administrative staff, house parents, and proctors. They were uniformly gracious as well as indispensable.

Norma Feshbach contributed to the design of the experiment and to the development of several of the instruments, as well as making a number of editorial suggestions. Edward Burke facilitated our initial contacts with the California institutions, and Roger Wickland, with the assistance of Gerald Senf, continued to maintain positive relationships with the participating institutions while helping supervise the day-to-day implementation of the experiment. Charles Woodson was of inestimable help in the data control phase, supervising the scoring and computer programing of the data as well as offering helpful statistical advice. Ted Nickel did an excellent job of filling in for Woodson after the latter completed his degree. William Stiles, Yoram Jaffe, and John Simpson spent many exacting hours transferring computer output to comprehensible tables, while Carol Pincus, Barbara Mooney, and Susan Fielding painstakingly typed the tables as well as the accompanying script. Will Fuller assisted in the proofreading and made a number of helpful suggestions.

The study was primarily carried out through the auspices of the Human Interaction Research Institute. They provided both autonomy and efficient administrative support. A number of the measuring instruments employed in this study were developed in connection with U.S.P.H.S. Grant MH 10973 awarded to the senior author and administered by the University of California, Los Angeles. That investigation is concerned with "The Organization and Regulation of Aggression." The authors are grateful for the support of this grant and the detailed analysis which it permitted. The senior author also wishes to acknowledge the help provided by a sabbatical quarter.

The basic funds for this project were provided in an award to the senior author by the Joint Committee for Research on Television and Children. The committee gave us complete freedom in carrying out the study, leaning over backwards in some instances in order to avoid any possible question of interference. Their interest and support are deeply appreciated.

Los Angeles   SEYMOUR FESHBACH
September 1970   ROBERT D. SINGER

Contents

TELEVISION
AND
AGGRESSION

An Experimental
Field Study

ONE

Aggressive Fantasies

Apparently well before recorded history men were fascinated by accounts of aggressive actions. The telling and retelling of the kill in an exciting hunt or the recounting of a bloody victory over an enemy tribe probably furnished many recitals over evening campfires. Pictures on cave walls, painted many thousands of years ago, include scenes of hunting and fighting, as do pictographs in the tombs of ancient Egyptian pharaohs. Folk tales, myths, and legends are rich in scenes of anger, hatred, murder, revenge, and battle. Homer, the Greek tragedians, the Bible, Shakespeare, Conrad, Hemingway, and Faulkner have all vividly described acts of divine and human violence. Aggression has always been one of the principal

1

themes of literature. Hardly any great play or novel does not partly depict scenes of hostility or acts of violence.

Preoccupation with aggression is not restricted to adult literature. Children's fairy tales and stories have their violent, frightening giants, grandmother-devouring wolves, cruel step-mothers, evil witches, and fiendish criminals. Actual or threatened pain, dismemberment, and death are commonplace in tales told for scores and possibly hundreds of years to children of many ages in many lands. As children become older they read about warrior heroes, pirates, brave fighting dogs, dashing swordsmen, and battles in outer space.

The presentation of violence for the enjoyment of children and adults comes in many forms, from Dickens' *Oliver Twist* to Tarzan and from Dead Eye Dick penny dreadfuls to Superman comics. In fact every conceivable means and combination of means of communication have been used. Although oral storytelling is the oldest form, pictorial modes of communication developed quickly and then the written word. Plays and dance forms made possible combinations of oral and visual pretended aggression. Printing per-mitted the communication of fantasy aggression to mass audiences, and illustrated books presented violence both verbally and pictori-ally. Radio provided still a new way of communicating aggressive themes. It was a mass oral medium, without face-to-face contact, which could reach millions of people. With it came "Gangbusters," "Captain Midnight," "Jack Armstrong," and "The Lone Ranger," not to mention individual broadcasts such as Orson Welles' "Inva-sion from Mars." Radio was followed by the movies, which permitted oral and visual presentation of violence to mass audiences. Movies began with films like *The Great Train Robbery*. Movies now seem to have reached an all time high in the depiction of aggression with such pictures as *Bullitt* and *The Wild Bunch*. In between, the public has enjoyed westerns, war movies, and horror and gangster films galore.

The last contender in the arena of the mass communication of fantasy aggression is television. Like the movies, television has exploited most known forms of mayhem. Cartoon animals and caricatured humans chase each other in an endless round of destruction and miraculous recovery from ingenious forms of annihilation. The Old West is littered with dead cowboys and Indians, while private eyes and super sleuths do battle with murderers and enemy agents. Submarines fight undersea monsters and spaceships zap alien intruders. Objection to such programs brought, starting in the 1969–1970 season, a decline in TV fantasy violence. However, in the eyes of some critics, the quality of television has shown little improvement since then. They contend that substitutes for the more violent shows or violent content are mainly trivial situation comedies or inferior dramas.

The communication of aggression is not restricted to the presentation of violence to people who passively absorb the message from some medium. People dream at night; they also have daydreams and the capacity to imagine in various ways (Singer, 1966). And they interact with or react to the forms and contents which reach them. The impact of books and radio depends, to a fair extent, on use of the imagination—that is, on the ability of people to make vivid for themselves the presented material. People very often supply their own visions of battles depicted in a book, and some even smell gunpowder or hear a distant cannon as part of the experience. Some people in their forties report preferring old radio programs like "I Love a Mystery," "Inner Sanctum," and "Green Hornet" to television programs because they could imagine the events and embellish them in fantasy.

What has been read or heard or seen may become part of a person's private fantasy life. A frightening fairy tale may lead to a child's nightmare. The tale of a courageous warrior may awaken fantasies of revenge on a disliked adult. Conversely, daydreams of being a great hunter may lead a man to enjoy some of Hemingway's short stories. People identify with heroes and villains in the world of aggressive entertainment; that is, in fantasy, they imagine themselves to be both the recipients and the producers of the actions and feelings depicted. Walter Mitty is perhaps the best known fictional character who vicariously lived the life of his imaginary heroes. The relationship between an individual and the aggression described in fictional form is interactive. Clearly, whatever its specific effects, the depiction of human violence produces results through stimulation of and interaction with the individual's fantasy life.

Fantasies have a number of elements, which may be reduced to three for the convenience of analysis. First, fantasies, particularly externally produced ones, involve sensory modalities, chiefly hearing and vision, but possibly other forms of perception such as kinesthetic sensations or even smell. Second, fantasies involve cognitions. That is, fantasies concern matters about which people are capable of thinking. The thought may be elaborate or simple, correct or in error, but they do involve elements which the person is capable of labeling in one way or another. Aggressive fantasies revolve around mothers, fathers, teachers, bosses, people of another race or religion, sisters, brothers. They can be about almost anyone or anything capable of at least some rudimentary depiction and description. Third, fantasies have an affective (emotional) component. Few fantasies are neutral; perhaps none are. They involve hope, joy, tension, relief, pleasure, fear, anger, hatred, and other feelings.

A distinction needs to be made between the occurrence or depiction of actual aggression and the presentation or production of aggressive fantasies. Very young children often probably do not make this distinction psychologically. That is, they may respond in the same way to actual and to fantasied aggression on their own part and in a highly similar way to needs and to thoughts about hurting people (Fenichel, 1945). However, children rapidly become capable of distinguishing reality and fantasy and do not react in the same way to both. Certain television programs, such as westerns, which initially frighten children soon lose their power to do so (Himmelweit, 1958). The stereotyped violence of westerns, unrelated to the child's everyday experiences, with repetition and advances in the child's age, ceases to scare him. Furthermore, no matter how real, the external communication of aggression cannot be expected to have effects equivalent to those which result from the exercise or experience of violence. Neither is the fantasy of aggression equivalent to the perpetration of violence. The reader or viewer does not get hurt, he is not in pain, he does not bleed or die. The child intently viewing mayhem on the TV set is not kicking anybody or bloodying his brother's nose. When the distinction between the carrying out of actual aggressive behaviors and the indulgence of aggressive fantasy is lost or blurred, one is likely to be dealing with a psychotic or otherwise quite disturbed person. Dick Gregory, the black comedian and civil rights leader, in his autobiography, *Nigger,* depicts vividly the violent aggressive fantasies engaged in by himself and a close childhood friend. However, he points out that the daydreams of violence were not acted out in reality. The aggression of the two boys never amounted to more than quite minor property damage.

In an equivalent way, children and adults are able to distinguish between the consequences of aggression in play or sport and the effects of violence in reality. The results of playing war with toy soldiers, playing cowboys and Indians, or punching a Bobo doll are one class of events, and the outcomes of such acts as kicking one's mother are quite another. Punching a bag, playing tackle football, hunting, and fishing are not equivalent to murder in their cognitive, emotional, or behavioral consequences for the individual. The reinforcing consequences, positive or negative, of fantasy or sport aggression are seldom equivalent to those of engaging in overt violence, and while under some conditions there is a functional equivalence between fantasy and reality, these cases still require additional empirical specifications.

Psychoanalytic literature comments on unfortunate situations which may occur in early childhood when the consequences of fantasy seem to be the same to the child as the consequences of overt acts. For instance, it has been claimed that a young child may blame himself if a relative dies after the child has engaged in hostile fantasies concerning that person. The consequence of the child's wish that the person die seems to be the same as that which would have followed if the child had actually carried out an act of violence, and he may experience a great deal of guilt. A child daydreams about obtaining a desired expensive toy, and he gets it. He may attribute the gift to his own magical powers. Possibly such occurrences early in childhood give rise to thinking about magic, beliefs in witchcraft, and exaggerated notions of one's own power (Brenner, 1955; Fraiberg, 1959).

However, most children do learn, to a fair extent, that wishing does not and will not make it so. They make distinctions between fantasies and overt acts not only through the aid of experience and perception of differential consequences but also with the help of direct explanation and action by adults. Pointing out and demonstrating to children that they have to work for what they want and showing them that problems need to be solved and cannot be wished away help to sharpen their knowledge of causality. Children's repeated interactions with the world as it exists also serve this purpose (Nunberg, 1955; Piaget, 1955).

In the mass media, the attempt to portray violence as real or imaginary varies markedly, as does the consequent ease of discrimination. Television, for instance, presents news, documentaries, and sports programs which involve acts of real violence. Strong efforts are made to convey the reality and veridicality of what is shown. There may be scenes of the war in Vietnam or of fighting between Arabs and Israelis. Part of a riot may be shown with fighting between students and the police, or the scene of a murder may be presented with a description of the crime. Such presentations are often highly realistic.

At the other end of the spectrum are such shows as "Batman" or "Get Smart," where violence is highly unreal and is presented in a caricatured manner or in humorous contexts. Also toward this end of the spectrum are formula westerns and similar programs whose actions and outcomes are predictable and whose villains and heroes are removed from modern experience. Not too far down the line come the various detective and spy programs and submarine and spaceship adventures.

Closest to reality are programs in which fantasy violence occurs but in which the actions of the fictional characters may be close to some experiences of the viewer. Situations in these programs are not unlike those which may occasionally occur in daily life. Consequently, violence or its threat, in shows like "Lassie" or in certain movies shown on TV like *Magnificent Obsession*, may have a strong emotional impact on the viewer. Seeing a dog in danger, a child being hurt, a man killing an animal, or a man threatening a woman with a knife in a kitchen reminds the child and even the adult of actual or potential situations which are real and meaningful to him. Such true to life scenes are the ones most upsetting to the viewer and most likely to lead to consequences such as nightmares (Himmelweit, 1958).

The effects of the depiction of real aggression on television are not clear. The extent to which adults and children distinguish among various gradations of what is meant to be fact or fantasy varies. Everything may seem equally real to the very young child, while some adults may fail to grasp the reality when seeing a video-tape of a napalm bursting in a Vietnamese village. Our discussion and the study to be presented in detail are restricted to the possible functions and effects of those TV programs whose intent is to be fictional.

Since the fantasy aggression which results from viewing these programs precedes recorded history and since individuals persist in their desire to consume such fantasies through the mass media, certainly fantasy serves some function. People not only persist in dreaming, daydreaming, and telling stories, but also read comics, buy novels, watch television, and go to movies. One may postulate a relatively constant need for fantasy activity since the time people spend in it seems to be fairly constant regardless of the media involved. If television is unavailable, there is more comic book reading or greater movie attendance. If television is readily available, then the consumption of other fantasy media declines. The total time spent in such fantasy activities, however, stays roughly the same (Schramm, Lyle, and Parker, 1961). Thus, we can assume that fantasies do something for people; otherwise they would not engage in them. To put it in more formal terms, fantasies have reinforcing effects. What, however, are the specific effects of engaging in fantasy activities? Why are these activities reinforcing? Do they satisfy esthetic, emotional, and cognitive needs exclusively or do they also relate to overt behavior?

Several explanations have been advanced concerning the role fantasy plays in relation to overt human behavior. Two of these are very closely related, both being derived from psychoanalytic theory. One states that fantasies are substitutes for desired but relatively unobtainable goal states (Freud, 1962a, 1962b; Seeman, 1951).

The other contends that fantasies lower states of tension or drive (Feshbach, 1955). In these views, sexual fantasies are a substitute when actual intercourse or the object of the fantasy is unavailable or unobtainable. Aggressive fantasies are substitutes for injuring someone when such action is inhibited by fear of external or internal retribution. Since sexual or aggressive arousal or drive is present, fantasies also partly lower the drive or tension. The degree of reward or satisfaction from substitute fantasy activities is less than the amount which could be obtained from overt sexual or aggressive behavior, and consequently only partial reduction of arousal or drive occurs.

Several propositions should follow if such explanations are correct. The more often and more quickly a person is able to fulfill his needs—that is, obtain rewarding stimuli—the less he should engage in fantasies. Conversely, the more often inhibitory forces or real or anticipated punishments deter the attainment of preferred goals, the greater the amount of fantasy. Delays between arousal of a motive and its satisfaction should also produce increased fantasies. For instance, frustration, often defined as delay in reaching reinforcing stimuli, should be a condition for the appearance of fantasy responses. In fact, psychoanalytic theory posits that the infant's first fantasy—that of the nipple when feeding is delayed—is a product of frustration and that a hallucination of the nipple is presumably better than no nipple at all.

Another view invokes principles of conditioning to explain the existence of fantasy activity. Chains of behavior such as those involved in sexual intercourse, striking an enemy, feeding, or drinking are usually accompanied by visual, olfactory, auditory, tactile, and other stimuli and are also associated with specific classes of thoughts. Overt behavior is probably also accompanied, on most occasions, by affective stimuli like pleasure, pain, and anger. The stimuli associated with various chains of behavior can be discriminated from each other so that sexual, feeding, and aggressive acts and their associated rewards are psychologically different from each other. In addition, the complex of perceptual, affective, and cognitive stimuli associated with these states vary and are discriminable. When stimuli begin to arouse the responses in a given chain of behavior, they also give rise to the fantasies representative of and usually part of the sequence of overt acts. If overt behavior is inhibited or if it is impossible because of the absence of a suitable goal (source of major reinforcement), the fantasy may continue and become the principal ongoing activity (Mowrer, 1960).

Since fantasies are often present just before or at the time of reward (such as orgasm, obtaining food, or striking an enemy), they may acquire rewarding properties. The mother may feed the child just after he has fantasied the nipple. An attacking child may just have imagined beating another boy. When hit, the other boy cries out in pain, turns, and flees. In such ways fantasies become associated both with rewarding acts and with the specific chains of stimulation leading up to them. Consequently fantasies are seen as partially satisfying and as helping to reduce strong stimulation or drives.

An associated but different concept views fantasy as a coping mechanism, chiefly cognitive in nature (Singer, 1966). The ability to engage in fantasies is seen as an adaptive function which helps the human organism to cope with the long periods during which primary reinforcements may not be available. For instance, the child who is frustrated but who has a vivid fantasy life is more able to cope than a frustrated child who does not have this ability. The former child is not driven to inappropriate disturbing behaviors, while the other child is likely to engage in such behaviors as social withdrawal and disorganized thinking. Some evidence shows that the imaginative child prone to fantasy is not likely to become psychotic, but the irritable, hyperactive child with little internal capacity to benefit from fantasy activity may develop serious mental problems.

Fantasy, in this view, stands as a protection between the internally aroused individual and his need to engage in possibly damaging external behavior. It is a control or coping mechanism which allows for delays in behavior (Meltzoff, Singer, and Korchin, 1953; Singer, 1960). Since part of any fantasy is cognitive, children who are more cognitively differentiated are better able to utilize fantasy in constructive ways than less cognitively differentiated children. Consequently variables like higher intelligence, upper middle class family background, provision of books, and time alone are productive of the ability to develop fantasy skills. Children with lower intelligence, a lack of books, impoverished stimulation, and no time to be alone or to think have less ability to fantasize (Singer, 1966). Possibly for such children television, comics, or movies provide readily understood fantasies which they are unable to manufacture for themselves.

There is also the contention, contrary to the views discussed above, that fantasies serve an arousing function rather than a reinforcing, drive-reducing, or coping function. Proponents of this position argue that fantasies, sometimes aroused by external cues, are often used as a goad to action. They point to phenomena like being aroused by a sexy movie, daydreaming about a girl friend, or having images of sexual activity as preliminary stages of arousal preceding sexual intercourse. Proponents of this position discuss the tendency of some groups, before a fight or battle, to work themselves up by recounting past victories, denigrating their enemies, and engaging in other fantasies concerning the encounter to come. According to this view the function of a fantasy is to arouse the individual and prepare him to engage in overt action.

Conditioning theory, interestingly enough, lends some currency to this outlook as well as to its opposite. If fantasies can and do occur at all points of an ongoing chain of behavior, they are associated with states of increasing arousal as well as with reinforcements and possible decrements in arousal. Since reinforcements and lowering of arousal are associated with goal attainment, fantasies occurring at that time may reduce arousal. Other fantasies, however, may be common at earlier stages of goal directed sequences when arousal is high and may therefore be associated more strongly with excitatory potential than with quiescence.

The beginning of a chain of aggressive activity may have associated with it images of obtaining a weapon and engaging in destructive violence. Such fantasies can be arousing because of repeated association with increasing activity which culminates in the reinforcement resulting from injuring someone. The fantasies common at the time someone is hurt, however, may reduce arousal. Consequently daydreaming about obtaining a knife to hurt someone may be arousing, while daydreaming about how the other person may look when he is stabbed and severely injured may be drive-reducing. In addition, fantasies involving severe injury may inhibit by producing fear and anxiety about the consequences of aggression. Thus, certain fantasies may be associated with high levels of responding or vigorous activity, while others are associated with low levels of responding preceding a change in activity or with inhibitory states. The former fantasies are partial causes of increases in activity (arousal), while the latter are partial causes of reduction in activity (drive reduction or inhibition).

To summarize, fantasies, in relation to behavior, have been cited as substitutes for overt behavior which are partly rewarding in themselves and which may reduce arousal, as coping or adaptive mechanisms useful when delays in gratification occur, and as aids to arousal possibly culminating in overt behavior. Probably fantasies can fill any of these functions. What the effects of a given fantasy are at any time depends on the other variables involved. We consider some of these variables later in this chapter. Although fantasies also have functions not necessarily related to overt social behavior (Humphrey, 1958), including various esthetic satisfactions largely limited to emotional and cognitive states which do not culminate in social acts with consequences for others, our discussions, in general, are limited to the relationship between fantasy aggression and overt behavior.

In discussions about this relationship, a great deal has been said about the effects of viewing violence on television, particularly about its effects on children. The statements however often tend to convey opinion rather than fact since little direct evidence bears on this question. Principal concern has been about the possible effects on the overt socially aggressive behavior of children. Certainly children watch many hours of TV richly filled with scenes of imaginary violence. The chief question is whether viewing such shows increases the probability that a child will injure another human being. Three answers are possible and all three have been given. The first is that viewing TV violence increases the probability that a child will engage in violence. The second is that, on the contrary, viewing such shows makes it less probable that a child will act aggressively toward others. The third is that the probabilities of a child's becoming overtly aggressive are not affected by his watching televised scenes of fantasy violence.

It is instructive to examine the rationale for each of these three positions. Many who decry the prevalence of violence in TV programing believe that such shows increase violence on the part of the viewer. First, they contend that children learn from television just as they learn from any visual-auditory display. There is ample evidence that such observational learning takes place, and it takes place often (Bandura, Ross, and Ross, 1963; Bandura and Walters, 1963). The presumption is that children learn techniques or methods of violence which would otherwise not come to their attention. The child may learn how to use a knife in a fight, how to pull the trigger of a gun, or how to hang someone by seeing it done on television. Then, when he is bent on hurting someone and a knife, gun, or rope is handy, he will use it. Or he may attempt to get such instruments in a manner observed earlier on television.

Second, it has been claimed that many programs have a general arousing effect which makes violence more probable. A variety of mechanisms suggest how this may happen. One involves the possibility that scenes of violence are simply exciting; they raise tension levels and attendant rates of activity, and an active child is more likely to hurt someone than is a quiet one. Among the many behavioral tendencies aroused in this process, some are certain to be aggressive. Furthermore, vigorous activity is likely to be injurious—pushes, shoves, and punches are simply vigorous forms of pats, touches, and taps. In fact, a response may be labeled aggressive because it is vigorous (Bandura and Walters, 1963).

A less direct avenue to this second possibility has also been suggested. Violent fantasy activity on television is believed to stimulate the child's own violent fantasies through identification. For instance, seeing a hero kill a villain on TV, the child may, some believe, imagine himself as a good guy punishing his "bad" brother. Having this fantasy increases the chance that he will shortly hurt his brother in some way. The child sees himself as being similar to someone who commits violence and sees the person he hurts as the deservedly injured party (Freud, 1937).

A third possibility is that witnessing aggressive action on television reduces the child's inhibitions against aggressive expression. An integral part of the socialization process which children undergo is the acquisition of controls over the expression of aggressive behavior. No culture could long survive if its members freely engaged in internecine aggressive activities. As Freud (1957) stressed, one of the costs of living in an organized society is the inhibition of free expression of aggressive impulses. The inhibitions inculcated by the culture take two major forms, prohibitions and anxieties, which the child has internalized, and the fear of punishment and the need to conform to norms of conduct, which are situationally dependent. Exposure to aggressive interactions on television, some argue, may weaken external restraints, especially if these actions meet with approval rather than with punishment. The child may get the message that it is all right to act aggressively, that shooting and beating are really not bad, that he will not be punished for what he had previously perceived as unacceptable behaviors (Bandura and Walters, 1963).

Since these three possibilities are not incompatible, one can combine the learning, the arousal, and the reduction of inhibition arguments. In this general incitement to aggression view, the child learns how to be aggressive from viewing television, is aroused to act out the techniques he has learned through TV and other media, and experiences little fear of punishment for giving overt expression to aggressive inclinations. The depiction of violence, therefore, is seen as a multifaceted evil.

In contrast, those who see fantasy largely either as a partly rewarding substitute for overt aggression or as an adaptive coping mechanism hold that watching television programs depicting violence may reduce the incidence of aggressive behavior on the part of the viewer. They assume that over time children and adults experience various instigations to behave aggressively and acquire various levels of aggressive response. Individuals may be deprived of things they want or not get them soon enough; they may be insulted, demeaned in some way, or even physically attacked. Under such circumstances they may resort to aggression. Furthermore, they may learn that aggression can be a means of obtaining desired resources, that force can be used instrumentally (Feshbach, 1970).

Neither adults nor children, however, behave violently every time they experience some instigation to aggression because a variety of constraints or inhibitory forces are usually present. Expectations of social disapproval, punishment, shame or guilt, and fear of retaliation tend to counterbalance the arousal tendencies to hurt others. Also, the use of aggression to gain desired ends may not succeed. Aggressive fantasies, in addition to memories of previous punishment for aggression, can lower the probability of violent action. With some inhibitions against aggression already present, the ability to fantasize the injury one wishes to inflict on others provides a partial satisfaction which somewhat lowers the level of instigation to attack. In these cases, a person may daydream about how he is going to tell off the boss, may dream at night about a symbolic revenge for some humiliation that he has experienced, or may doodle explosions, guns, and knives while a long and boring lecture is keeping him from lunch.

As suggested earlier, fantasy activities may possibly work in several ways to lower the probability that a violent act will occur. First, there may be a direct effect on level of arousal. If a person is very angry—that is, affectively aroused—fantasy activity may reduce anger and thus the level of arousal. If the source of instigation to aggression is sufficiently punished in fantasy, then the goal of inflicting injury has been partly fulfilled and the level of arousal (drive) is lowered. Second, to the extent that the individual is rewarded through fantasy, behaviors other than acting aggressively (chiefly the behavior of engaging in fantasies) are reinforced. Repeated occurrences of fantasy activity leading to a reinforcing state strengthen the tendency (or habit) of fantasizing. If aggressive tendencies are aroused in the future the individual may turn at once to some preferred fantasy rather than attacking. Clinical accounts tell of overly passive children who almost never engage in aggressive behavior but who instead entertain all sorts of violent fantasies (Kessler, 1966).

Third, violent scenes on television or in other media may provide fantasy material usable by the viewer. He may perceive fictional characters as being similar to himself and to intended victims. He may, while viewing or afterward, utilize the depicted scenes as fantasy materials to lower his state of arousal and to partially substitute for overt behavior.

Fourth, viewing television violence may also lead to a decrease in aggressive behavior through inhibition. It may frighten the viewer of violence and its possible consequences; it may create over aggressive impulses and the eventuality that they may be acted out. The viewer consequently avoids aggressive behavior in order to reduce his fear of what he may do or what may be done to him (Berkowitz, 1964).

Fifth, television fantasy aggression may also provide the materials needed for cognitive control of behavior. If the ability to engage in fantasy is seen as an adaptive, coping mechanism, then people with a relatively low fantasy ability may need to have fantasy material provided from external sources. Thus, middle class, highly intelligent, and cognitively well developed children would not derive much benefit from viewing TV fantasy violence. Such children should be able to manufacture their own fantasy life from everyday experience, imaginative elaboration, and occasional contact with presentations of fictional aggression. Children or adults with a limited intelligence and a low capacity for imagination, however, may have to rely heavily on external sources of fantasy material.

A question arises as to the nature of the fantasies that help people cope with situations in which there are both instigation to aggression and also good reasons not to attack. Does any mental activity engaged in after instigation to aggression alter the individual's psychological state in such a way as to make aggressive behavior less probable? Do fantasies of sexual activity, of obtaining wealth, or of other pleasant distractions serve an adaptive purpose as well as or better than aggressive fantasies do? Such nonviolent acts of imagination have the advantage of being substitute distractions incompatible with violence and are not open to the charge that violent fantasies are themselves instigations to violence. Such nonaggressive fantasies may also induce change to a mood incompatible with aggression. One is reminded of the old burlesque joke of the man about to spank his wife who forgot that he was angry as soon as he lifted her skirt. If it is a question only of developing alternate, nonviolent means of coping with aggressive instigation, then a variety of nonaggressive fantasies may serve that function; many quite different imaginative activities may help decrease the probability that aggressive behavior will occur.

The alternate possibility is that for fantasies to be of optimal use in coping with situations, they must be reasonably related in content to those situations. Fantasies are not wholly wish-fulfilling and devoid of reality aspects. There is no complete separation between thinking directed to problem solution and fantasy activity (Singer, 1966). Fantasies may provide the materials necessary for reaching reward or for avoiding punishing consequences. To accomplish this goal, they need to bear some relation to the problem at issue. Consequently fantasy material related to aggression would, in this view, be more helpful in aiding a person to cope with instigations to violence than would other fantasy materials. Nonaggressive fantasy scenes may be distracting or may induce changes in mood, thus reducing the possibility of violence, but, it can be argued, they do not lead to overt coping behaviors and they are less likely to be evoked by aggressive stimuli than are fantasies with aggressive content. A very angry person will probably not turn to daydreams about money.

A final view is that fantasy activity or exposure to various sorts of violence through the mass media is largely irrelevant to the occurrence of aggressive behavior. In such a view the chief determinants of aggression are instigating and reinforcing variables. The level of aggression is a combined outcome of arousal, reward, and punishment, and the principal sources of arousal are events which generally or specifically increase the vigor of aggressive responding. These events include those usually considered to be frustrating or related to anger and similar states. If aggression leads to a reinforcing state, it will be likely to recur in the future (Sears and others, 1953). The chief reinforcers of aggression are avoiding injury, as in self-defense; obtaining nonaggressive goals, such as possessions, through violence; and inflicting injuries on others. The principal variables operating to prevent aggression are lack of positive reinforcement and occurrence of punishment. In this view people are aggressive when they want something that can be obtained by using violence and when they wish to hurt someone. People refrain from violence because it may get them nothing and because it may lead to being punished by others or to self-disapproval.

Proponents of this view see fantasy as a negligible source of variance affecting violent behavior. They admit that television programs do cause some arousal or lowering of aggressive drive and that they may also serve some minimal positively reinforcing and inhibitory functions. However, they believe that such effects are at best trivial in the determination of behavior in the general population. The consequences chiefly determine how people act. Humans are socially aggressive to the extent that tendencies to aggression are aroused and aggression brings reward. People are nonaggressive to the degree that aggression brings them nothing or brings them undesired effects (is negatively reinforcing) and to the degree that frustration and anger are kept at a minimum. Proponents of this position are usually not overly impressed with the role of emotional or cognitive factors in the determination of social behavior. They see how people behave toward each other, including how violent they are with each other, as a function of how the world treats various social behaviors. If the enviroment allows violent acts to succeed, they will recur; if it does not, they will decline. Thus, behavior is almost exclusively under the control of external events and consequences and is only negligibly, if at all, under the guidance of inner states like fantasies or the perception of fantasy in the media (Premack, 1965).

Proponents of this viewpoint contend that since man is a cognitive animal and an emotional one, he may well be fascinated by aspects of his own behavior and the exercise of his capacities. He may like to think about what is important to him, whether it is sex, affection, violence, or accomplishment. He may fantasize about such matters of importance or write about them or paint pictures or make movies or television shows to depict them. However, they believe that such activities are ends in themselves, good or bad, enjoyable or not, related to how people think and feel and not to what they do. Violence on television, in their view, neither adds to nor detracts from the sum of human aggression.

Some individuals who are opposed to the repeated depiction of violence on television are not concerned chiefly with the possibility that the adult viewer will himself go out and shoot a neighbor or that the child who enjoys "Batman" will kick the family dog. Many critics of what they consider excessive programing of violence are well aware of the social constraints which usually keep children and adults alike from injuring each other often or seriously. They are more concerned with the attitudes which television may be inculcating and the emotional responses which it may be engendering. Specifically, they point to the fact that most television programs involving violence include a good guy or guys who, in the name of "my" country, "our" side, or law and order, inflict injury or death on the bad guys. Such programs, they feel, inculcate attitudes to the effect that it is all right for "our" sheriffs, "our" policemen, "our" detectives, "our" generals, "our" submarines and spaceships to injure and kill anyone labeled bad or not on "our" side. The messages seem to be that violence is the best method for fighting violence and that aggression is justified if used against people considered to be deserving of punishment. Ironically, the person or group to be demolished is usually designated as the aggressor. The result of being exposed to such attitudes, it is argued, is not particularly violence on the part of the viewer but the increased probability that he will support, condone, or justify aggression on the part of his own police department or armed forces. Alternative possibilities to violence, according to this view, are less likely to be considered since they are seldom presented.

The second effect posited is the possibility that continued exposure to violence erodes emotional revulsion to aggression. After seeing continued fantasy violence on television almost daily for years, the viewer is said to become calloused and indifferent to mayhem. Death and dismemberment, it is argued, lose their ability to shock; fear and empathy decline, while violence loses its reality. Analogies are drawn to the accounts of people whose chief function was to torture others. Such persons were at first terribly upset and revolted by their own brutal behavior toward others but, in the course of

time, became inured and finally were able to inflict the most ago-
nizing pain on people with little apparent feeling.

Both of these two arguments depend to a considerable extent
on the proposition that children and adults do not make reasonably
sharp distinctions between the world of fiction and the world of
reality. The implicit assumption is that attitudes and feelings about
violence are, in many instances, shaped as strongly by westerns,
detective stories, or other adventure series as by experiences with
actual violence or by religious teachings, education, or other attempts to cope with social and political reality. It is particularly
claimed that fictional portrayals or word of mouth remarks are effec-
tive in shaping attitudes toward matters with which people have
little direct experience. If people seldom interact with Indians, com-
munists, foreign officials, or hippies, portraying them as aggressive,
nasty, and worthy of punishment has a strong effect. Not having
much experience as a guide, people may see fictional portrayals as
tantamount to reality. All sorts of violent fantasies may then be
entertained about groups with which the viewing public seldom
interacts. These fantasies, translated into attitudes, are then said to
form the basis for the tacit permission given to various public authorities to deal severely with certain people such as hippies, com-
munists, or radical students.

Finally, objections to televised violence have been raised not
on the grounds of the harm it may do but on the grounds that viewing time could be put to much better use. Programs revolving
around aggressive themes have in the past accounted for a good
deal of this time. Most of these programs are said to have little
artistic or educational merit. It has been vigorously contended that
the viewing public would be better off if the punching, kicking, and
shooting were replaced by serious plays, symphony concerts, ballets,
modern and popular music, discussions of social problems, and other
educational programs. The gist of the argument is that not being
bad is not good enough. The heavy programing of fantasy violence
is apparently seen as undesirable at least partly because it takes up
time better devoted to other activities and subjects (Himmelweit,
1958). However, the real complaint is about television shows in
general and not about violence in particular. A temporary decline

of television fantasy aggression has brought replacements consisting of comedies about bachelor fathers, millionaire hillbillies, and frontier mothers, supplemented by quiz games, soap operas, comedians, and popular singers. These programs are not likely to please the critics of television more than the former load of mayhem did.

It is not possible to comprehend the possible effect of exposure to fantasy violence without some exploration of the nature of aggression. Human aggression can be analyzed into a number of categories, but for our purposes it will suffice to consider two general types. The first has been termed instrumental aggression and the second hostile aggression. The distinction is useful, but seldom does either type exist in a pure form. In the case of instrumental aggression, injury to others is carried out chiefly for the purpose of obtaining some other end. That is, violence is instrumental to the attainment of land, power, money, sexual enjoyment, or some goal other than injury. The bank robber who kills a guard standing between him and the cash drawer, the bombardier who drops explosives on the village below, or the child who pushes a playmate off his tricycle may be less intent on inflicting injury than on being rich, helping to win the war, or riding instead of walking. The element of anger or hostility may be minimal when aggression is the avenue to other gratification or to the carrying out of an obligation. In such cases not the infliction of injury but the attainment of some other desired end is the chief source of reinforcement (Feshbach, 1964). In hostile aggression the primary source of satisfaction (reinforcement) is the injury done to some person or group of people. Such aggressive behavior contains emotional, cognitive, and action components. There is anger or rage, some conception, however meager or distorted, of the disliked target, and an overt act of violence. The chief goal is to hurt someone either physically or psychologically (Feshbach, 1964).

Forces mitigate against appearances of the pure case. People find it difficult to engage in purely instrumental aggression. Since violence is considered to be wrong or undesirable unless justified, it is easier to injure people for the sake of profit or some other gain if one can dislike them or become angry with them. If the victims can be perceived as evil, stupid, inferior, or otherwise reprehensible, then one can be angry with them, and injuring them becomes a source of reinforcement in itself. The aggressor can feel vindicated and profit by his violent actions. Conversely, much hostile aggression involves personal gain beyond the rewards derived from injuring others. The Nazis were quite careful to confiscate the property of Jews including the gold fillings from the teeth of their corpses. Acts of violence against Negroes not only may fill sadistic needs but are instrumental in maintaining the social and economic position of the aggressor.

One of the utilities of the distinction between instrumental and hostile aggression involves the ascription of aggressive drive only to instances of predominantly hostile aggression. Aggressive drive is said to be present only if the source of reinforcement for aggression is the perception of or information concerning actual or symbolic injury to the property or person of the individual attacked. No aggressive drive is assumed to be present in the case of relatively pure instrumental aggression, although other drives may be operating (Feshbach, 1964).

Not all psychologists interested in aggression posit a drive construct. Some view aggression in Skinnerian fashion as consisting simply of a class of defined operants. That is, they class certain behavioral responses as aggressive and give primary attention to the acquisition of this class of responses as a function of reinforcement (Lovaas, 1961b; Cowan and Walters, 1963). They are also concerned with the frequency of occurrence of these responses and with their extinction as a function of schedules of reinforcement. Another issue is the way in which discriminative stimuli come to control the appearance of responses classed as aggressive. As is usual in the Skinnerian and related traditions, no statement is made as to the reinforcing event or events responsible for increasing the frequency of aggressive responding. In some studies carried out in this tradition, for instance, candy and verbal approval have been used as reinforcers to increase the frequency of aggressive behavior. There is no reason why, in this viewpoint, the perception of injury to another cannot be an important reinforcing event (stimulus). Whether it is would be a matter for empirical determination.

For those who feel it important to posit an aggressive drive,

drive reduction is the chief reinforcing event which increases the probability of future occurrences of aggressive behavior. Since the drive component is usually seen as containing a heavy affective loading of anger or rage, several consequences follow. When the aggressor succeeds in harming another person or his property, drive should diminish. Successful aggression leads to a drop in anger or rage, a diminishing of aggressive drive. However, at the same time, the very lowering of drive level reinforces the aggressive behavior which occurred. Drive is lower, leading to lowered instigation, but aggressive habit or the probability of behaving aggressively under any renewed future instigation is raised (Feshbach, 1964).

The theoretical propositions outlined above have important implications for the possible effects of fantasy aggression on aggressive behavior. If aggressive fantasies can lower aggressive drive, then instigation to aggression will be lowered (Feshbach, 1955). In addition, the behavior reinforced by drive reduction is not overt aggression but, rather, the act of fantasizing. If fantasy lowers aggressive drive and its anger or rage components, it also reinforces the response events present at the time of drive reduction. These response events consist not of acts of injuring someone but of acts of imagination. Thus, fantasy aggression is the class of responses whose probability is increased by the rewards produced by fantasies.

The habit strength of overt aggression or the operant strength of aggressive responses, to use alternative constructs, would not be affected by the reniforcement of aggressive fantasies. However, strong tendencies to engage in aggressive thoughts and imagery might come to serve as substitutes for overt aggression. If aggressive fantasy can be seen as a response partly incompatible with overt aggression, then the tendency to imagine attacking people, if stronger than the tendency to overtly attack them, may prevent overt aggression. People who have experienced stronger satisfactions from imagining what they would like to do to others than from doing it may engage in aggressive fantasies rather than in attack. Alternately, the inability to imagine hurting others may remove a form of substitute behavior that could serve as an alternative to overt attack. However, as discussed earlier, to the extent that aggressive fantasies tend to raise aggressive drive they may facilitate overt aggression.

Another aspect of aggression is its instinctual component. Only a simplified and brief discussion of this issue can be undertaken here. Several theoretical positions postulate a lesser or greater amount of instinctual causation of aggressive behavior. The most extreme position is that there is an aggressive instinct operating on an independent somatic basis and pressing constantly for discharge through aggressive behavior (Freud, 1927). An intermediary position states that the potential for aggression is constantly present on an instinctual basis but is elicited only when certain environmental events are present—frustration, an intruder, a sexual rival (Lorenz, 1966). Views positing a partial instinctual explanation of aggression hold that certain components of aggression such as anger or kicking are unlearned. However, whether these unlearned components are expressed in behavior is seen as dependent on learning.

The most extreme learning positions state that behaviors which cause injury to others are learned in the same way that other behaviors are. That is, they first arise because of observational learning, imitation, trial and error, or rather random activity, and become frequent or probable if they are reinforced (Bandura and Walters, 1963). Less extreme positions take into consideration the reflexive and maturational aspects of biting, kicking, striking out with the hands, and thrashing about. They may also consider anger and rage as partially unconditioned affective responses elicited by certain classes of unconditioned stimuli. Such positions treat certain components of aggression as relatively innate but concentrate on the role of learning, chiefly imitation and reinforcement, as a determiner of when, where, and how frequently such behavioral components occur in sequences of behavior involving injury to others.

From the extreme instinctual theory one would deduce that any form of aggression would tend to lower, but only temporarily, the instinctual pressure to inflict injury. Not all activities involving some aspect of aggression could be considered equally potent in relieving instinctual tension. Fantasy aggression would be less powerful than overt attack but still capable of bringing about some lowering of the need to cause injury. The extreme learning position would give no role to aggressive fantasy in determining the probability and frequency of overt aggression unless it were viewed as a strong incompatible response. Fantasy aggression would have an intermediary role in the less extreme instinctual or learning views. Its principal role would be in the regulation of aggressive drive through its partly innate but conditionable anger and rage components. The possibility of substituting aggressive fantasy for overt aggression and the question of the reinforcing value of imaginative aggression would then be issues for empirical test.

Consideration of the effects of television fantasy violence on aggressive behavior, viewed in the light of the theoretical alternatives presented in this chapter, is certainly complex. Television programs involving violence are quite variable. The content varies. The outcomes of aggression vary. The characters attacking and attacked differ. The programs do not present phenomena easily described in terms of clearly specified variables which are easily measurable and which occur in orderly sequences. The child or adult watches a variety of programs to differing extents in different circumstances over various time and age periods. It is useful to consider theories, but conclusions drawn on a theoretical basis are no substitute for empirical research on the effects of watching television under conditions quite similar in all ways possible to the experiences which people have with television.

TWO

Review of
Current Thinking

No single study can hope to fully discover what effects viewing televised fantasy violence has on overt aggressive behavior. The effects may differ for males and females, for adults, adolescents, and young children. The degree and type of aggression that may result from such exposure may vary with the amount of time spent viewing and the particular types of programs viewed. Level of intelligence, social class, or cognitive complexity of the viewer may be important. Furthermore, these viewer characteristics may interact with program characteristics in determining the ultimate effects, if any, of televised fantasy violence. Major alarm about the effects of depicting fantasy aggression on television centers on

25

its possible influence on children. The current study deals with pre-adolescent and adolescent boys. The focus was on boys because the issue of violence has been more germane to male behavior.

The question of sex differences in aggression has been extensively considered elsewhere (Feshbach, 1970; Maccoby, 1966) and will be only briefly noted here. Certainly by the beginning of elementary school girls have learned to be less overtly aggressive than boys. This socialization takes place through direct and symbolic modeling as well as through reinforcement of appropriate sex behaviors. Children also acquire an identity, a set of cognitions about themselves which state that they are girls, females, and destined to be mothers, or boys, males, and destined to be fathers. A part of the sex-typed role of girls consists of cognitive self-attributions incompatible with overt aggressive behavior such as punching or rock throwing. These cognitions are mediational in nature, exerting a directing influence over overt behavior. There is also the possibility that innate biological factors such as lesser strength and smaller bone structure make overt aggression a less rewarding behavior choice for females. Boys, in comparison, acquire a more aggressive behavioral pattern and develop an identity and sex-typed role behaviors partly compatible with acts of aggression under certain socially defined circumstances. The role prescriptions assigned to boys require them to fight back if attacked, to protect their sisters or younger brothers, and to retaliate if their family, religion, or race is slandered. Again, the male of the species may have a biological disposition to violence greater than that of the female; for example, there is evidence of a link between aggression and the male sex hormone. Such biological tendencies, if they exist, are reinforced by the socialization process and are also channeled and regulated by it (Singer and Singer, 1969).

Preadolescence and adolescence are periods of particular social concern in the study of aggression. During this period attention focuses most sharply on acts of delinquency involving violent behavior. The aggression of the young child is a concern chiefly to the family, the neighbors, or the local school. The primary school child may violate the law, but his acts are usually restricted to petty theft and minor property damage. By the junior high school years, however, the boy is strong enough to be a serious threat to life and property if he acts aggressively, particularly if he acts in concert with other boys. By about the age of twelve boys are strong and capable of systematically acting with others in gang wars, of using knives and other weapons for extorting money from children, of mugging, of purse snatching, and similar crimes. They are also more likely to engage in direct defiance of and aggression against authority. Although many acts of delinquency such as burglary or car theft are not in themselves aggressive, the perpetrators of such acts may resort to violence when apprehended (Singer and Singer, 1969).

Consequently, there is a great deal of interest in any factor which may significantly increase the probability that adolescent boys will engage in overt aggression. It has been suggested, indeed stated quite bluntly, that television programs portraying fantasy violence are an important cause of violent behavior in adolescent boys. This same charge has been made in the past concerning comic books. For this reason and because of methodological considerations, this group is of primary interest in the current study.

Nevertheless, in reviewing the existent state of knowledge related to the main area of investigation, it may be useful to consider a variety of studies concerning children of various ages. Certainly children begin viewing television well before early adolescence. Since television is an audiovisual medium, it also seems relevant to examine investigations which did not involve television but which did involve the effects of visual and auditory displays of aggressive behavior on the actions of observing children.

All studies, including the present one, have certain limitations. Research with humans embraces more uncertainties than research with physical objects or with animals. A physiological psychologist is currently investigating how birds acquire the characteristic vocal patterns of their species (Petrinovitch, 1970). In this procedure eggs are taken from nests and hatched in an incubator in a laboratory. Full control is exercised over all forms of stimulation reaching the newly hatched birds, that is, the psychologist dictates the history of his subjects as far as that history is a function of experience. The reasons for, as well as the strengths of, such controlled and manipulational animal experimental research are familiar to most psychologists and other behavioral scientists (Bachrach, 1962; Scott and Wertheimer, 1962).

However, the human subjects of any survey, clinical study, or experiment arrive with vast previous histories and extensive behavioral repertoires over which the investigator has had no control and about which, at best, he can have only incomplete knowledge. To speak metaphorically, the human subject is an addict. He is already addicted to television, to reading (if he is over six), to fantasizing, to behaving aggressively, to learning, to imitating, and to thinking and feeling. The effects of any new conditions to which a human being is subjected are partially a function of existing predispositions which are largely determined by previous learning history. In addition, the behavior of organisms is also a function of the actual circumstances to which they are exposed (Epstein, 1962).

Past history cannot be controlled to any great extent in studies utilizing humans, but the degree of current control exercised varies, depending on the method of investigation chosen. (Of course, the amount of knowledge about past experience also varies.) Three main avenues of research have been used to assess the possible effects of televised fantasy violence on aggressive behavior. These are the clinical method, correlational methods, chiefly involving surveys, and experiments in the laboratory or in the field. The clinical method attempts to elicit knowledge of past experience but is usually limited to what the subject is capable of communicating about his past. The clinician does not strive for current control; that is, he generally does not ask his client to watch more television or less or to indulge in greater or lesser fantasy in order to observe how behavior varies. The clinician is typically limited to making deductions about causality from the verbal and nonverbal communications of his client. Such deductions are not open to verification. Different clinicians are quite capable of coming to varying conclusions on the basis of identical or similar clinical data. The strength of the clinical method is the opportunity it provides to explore certain psychological phenomena in depth and to suggest important variables and hypotheses which should be investigated. Much current investigatory work in personality and abnormal psychology has its roots in the observations of practicing clinicians.

The correlational method is used to establish the degree to which two variables tend to vary together, but it often does not lend itself easily to the establishment of causal or functional relationships. It is more useful for predictive purposes than for positing functional relationships. Surveys, which utilize the correlational statistical method, may reveal that American adolescents of Chinese ancestry are seldom arrested by the police. As long as conditions do not change, this observation enables one to predict accurately that most groups of Chinese-American adolescents will have low arrest records. It does not explain why. Surveys can give us information about past history and current conditions. Such studies usually rely on correlational statistical analyses. Respondents to surveys, for instance, can give reasonably accurate information about which television shows they watch and how often. Information can also be gathered on the general adjustment of the viewers. To a less accurate extent, respondents also are able to answer questions about some of their past behaviors such as child rearing and about early life experiences. However, answers to such questions are much less reliable than one would wish (Hoffman and Lippitt, 1960). People may distort memories in a socially desirable direction or simply fail to remember accurately.

The experimental method is most useful in the verification of hypotheses, that is, in establishing functional or causal relationships. It allows the experimenter to vary one or more independent variables and to observe the effects on one or more dependent variables. When such studies are conducted in the laboratory, the chances that uncontrolled or unknown sources of variation will occur are at a minimum. Of course, the possibility always exists that the experimenter is inadvertently communicating to the subjects how he wishes them to behave or is unable to control some other important condition which is the real cause of the obtained results. A major problem in laboratory experimentation is the tendency of some investigators to make unwarranted extrapolations from the obtained results or to investigate variables which exist in the laboratory but not in the real world. The fact that children in a laboratory setting imitate aggressive play with toys or that college sophomores in the laboratory give more electric shocks if they see a gun has led some to assume that watching fantasy aggression on television induces children to injure others. Such assumptions may be in error, since the only valid basis for extrapolating from a laboratory setting to a naturalistic one is that the one is an adequate model of the other. The experimental studies done to date make no attempt to meet this condition. What determines behavior in the controlled laboratory setting may not control it in many naturalistic situations (Willems and Raush, 1969).

Although the laboratory experimental method is useful in establishing causal relationships, it has inherent limitations in predicting behavior in actual situations simply because in the natural world multiple variables operate simultaneously and the behavioral outcome is some function of the combined forces involved. Surveys or laboratory experiments may be able to establish most of the theoretical relationships involved in determining the occurrence of aggressive responses. However, such data can help us to predict accurately the probability that violence will occur in an extralaboratory setting only if it is possible to specify the presence and strength of all pertinent relationships and the results of their interaction in the naturalistic setting. This specification is seldom possible without direct study of the nonlaboratory situation.

Field experiments in naturalistic settings help overcome some limitations of the laboratory experiment. Although possibly less useful as a tool for isolating the effects of well-described single variables or as a method for establishing abstract scientific laws, this method may sometimes be superior for practical prediction. Since all pertinent variables may not be known or may not be capable of laboratory replication, some investigations may best be conducted where the major dependent phenomena of interest occur. The degree of control is almost always less, but that is the price paid for utilizing a number of interacting variables and conducting research where behavior occurs naturally. Watching televised fantasy violence is not a single variable but embraces a multitude of variables generated by a variety of people watching an array of programs. The effects, if any, occur under conditions not easily duplicable in the laboratory. The choice of research methods, of course, is intrinsically linked to one's purpose. If the purpose is to approximate naturalistic conditions so that predictions can be made about naturalistic behavior, then the field experiment may be the method of choice. If the aim is to isolate single functional relationships in order to build scientific laws, then the field experiment may be a relatively inefficient tool. If the goal is to establish the relative frequency with which certain people watch specific programs, then a survey may suffice.

Clinical studies of the effects of viewing television on behavior are rare. Some clinicians have contended that violence portrayed in comic books or on television increases aggressive behavior and is a major cause of delinquency (Wertham, 1954). However, such conclusions are usually by-products of clinical work. Clients do not enter a therapeutic relationship to be cured of reading comics or of viewing television. The intent of the clinician is to deal with the problems of the client and not to make a study of the effects of fantasy materials. Nevertheless, some clinicians feel that certain communications made by their clients in the course of therapy indicate that exposure to violent fantasy is a cause of aggressive behavior. Such inferences cannot be considered valid without empirical tests, but they certainly are hypotheses for testing. Clinical observations antedating both comic books and television suggest contrary hypotheses. The classical psychoanalytic view of hostile fantasies is that they are wish-fulfilling substitutes for action or unavailable goals and produce substitute gratification and a partial lowering of drive states (Freud, 1925). These are also propositions to be verified, and experiments have in fact been devised and carried out to test the drive-reducing function of fantasy activity (Feshbach, 1955, 1961).

Survey studies tend to compare either children who watch television with those who do not (because sets or stations are unavailable in their area) or children who watch a considerable amount of television with those who watch less television (Himmelweit, 1958; Schramm, Lyle, and Parker, 1961). The opportunity to compare nonwatchers to watchers is now almost totally absent in North America, England, and most of Europe, since stations and sets are so prevalent. Amount of watching and types of shows watched become the main independent variables. Sex, age, and socioeconomic class are common ways of classifying viewers. Among the dependent behavioral variables studied are fear shown, social adjustment, emotional disturbance, aggressive tendencies, sociability, time spent in activities such as reading or doing homework, and academic success. The general attempt is to show the degree of correlation (association) between the independent and dependent variables. Of course the relationships found can be stated only as associations since the variables are not under experimental control. In general, the association between the types of shows watched (and how much they are watched) and behavioral variables is studied.

An English study compared preadolescent and adolescent children who had television available at home with those who did not and did not watch regularly elsewhere. The survey also compared children into whose area television was introduced with another group of children whose area was still without television. It was found that some programs were occasionally frightening to a substantial minority of the children. However, there were no significant differences between viewers and nonviewers on measures of aggression, delinquency, and maladjustment. English television at that time did have children's shows which contained fantasy violence, both adventure story programs and serious plays with some violent content (Himmelweit, 1958). However, English children did not have the wide choice of channels and the great variety of violent programing which for years have been available to American children, and it may be argued that these results are not applicable to American children.

An American survey study reported that middle class children who were heavy consumers of fantasy material on television exhibited more antisocial aggression than middle class children who read more and watched less television. The relationship was not found for children in lower socioeconomic groups. The TV-fantasy–oriented middle class children appear to have experienced greater frustrations than the other groups did, as reflected by a great deal of conflict with parents and peers (Schramm, Lyle, and Parker, 1961). Several explanations can be offered for these results: Frequent watching of violent television programs may induce some middle class children to behave aggressively. Or frustrated and consequently aggressive middle class children who do not get along with parents or peers may seek in television the satisfactions they cannot obtain in everyday life. Or television may reduce some of the extreme aggressive tendencies which contribute to the children's difficulties. Or these children may be socially inadequate and able to engage in social activity only vicariously through television. Or watching violence on television may partially justify the children's own aggressive behavior and lower conflict over aggression by giving many examples of people being aggressive. Other explanations are possible and more than one of the above may be correct, but unfortunately survey results are often open to a variety of explanations and seldom allow for conclusive statements concerning functional relationships.

The survey method often involves a large scale study utilizing questionnaires. However, we are here using the term in the wide sense of any study whose results are chiefly treated correlationally and depend on the analysis of nonexperimentally produced associations between variables. Whether interviews, tests, or observations are used to gather the data, essentially a survey is made and a correlational method is involved in analyzing the results. Some survey studies have a partial, although indirect, bearing on the possible relationship of viewing TV fantasy violence and aggressive behavior. Two studies report that high frustration levels are associated with a preference for violent and action programs (Riley and Riley, 1951; Bailyn, 1959). Aggressive personality predispositions in boys have also been found to be associated with a preference for aggressive content in pictorial media. Boys who like aggressive hero material tend to be emotionally disturbed, to blame others, and to come from unstable families (Bailyn, 1959; Eron, 1963). Aggressive third grade boys tend to prefer violent television programs, although they may not watch television frequently. (None of these findings seem to hold with any consistency or to any important degree for girls.) These results are interpretable as evidence that aggressive television programs are rewarding for frustrated, maladjusted, and aggressive children. They might also be interpreted as evidence that aggression is aroused by violent programs. One possible interpretation is that partially disturbed children find some solace in hostile TV fantasy. Such programs may lower their aggressiveness and reduce frustration and tension. Alternately, it may be argued that such programs further isolate the child and become substitutes for social activity. They may elicit violent fantasies which may be acted out in socially aggressive behavior. Both general explanations may have some credibility, with the net resultant effects on behavior difficult to predict. No firm conclusions can be reached without further research.

Experimental manipulation of visual or audiovisual stimuli, simulating motion pictures or television, provides some information about the behavioral consequences of exposure to audiovisual media. Such studies have also helped to delineate some of the psychological processes through which the stimuli portrayed in movies or on television might mediate the behavior of the child. A pertinent study used twelve boys and twelve girls aged four and five as subjects. Pairs of children were exposed at different times to each of two cartoon films, one highly aggressive and one nonaggressive. Each pair of children was then allowed to remain in a room with no one else present. They were observed after each film exposure in order to record the amount of aggression shown and to measure any signs of guilt or anxiety exhibited. The children were not aware that adults were watching and recording their behavior, and the room contained a variety of toys, some aggressive (rubber dagger) and some not aggressive (toy telephone) in nature. The principal measure was the difference in aggression shown by the children after viewing nonaggressive and aggressive cartoons. The difference in scores proved to be insignificant; that is, there were no reliable differences in aggression, anxiety, or guilt shown by the children as a function of observing aggressive or nonaggressive cartoons (Siegel, 1956). This study has the merit of making observations on children playing together in a room with toys, an arrangement which simulates the naturalistic situations in which children frequently find themselves. Aggression was possible not only toward the toys (or self) but also toward another child who could be hurt and who could retaliate. This study did not support the hypothesis that viewing aggressive fantasy materials increases aggressive behavior.

Some caution needs to be used in citing this experiment as proof that television fantasy does not affect aggression. Exposure to the film cartoons was neither lengthy nor frequent, and possibly, even if a few programs have no effect, there is an effect from the multiple exposures over time. A second and related point is that the aggression level of the children in the experiment was to a fair extent a function of how aggressive they were in other situations; that is, their habitual level of aggression was the best predictor of how aggressive they were in the study. Finally, several other studies employing observation of an aggressive cartoon as the critical experimental variable have shown evidence of an increase in aggression following exposure (Lovaas, 1961a; Mussen and Rutherford, 1961).

The habitual level of aggression shown by a child in a given situation can be viewed as a predisposition. Some experimental studies show that what children learn from audiovisual media is a joint function of content and the dispositions of the child. These dispositions may be more or less permanent, as the habitual level of aggression, or temporary, as the short term arousal when a child has been mildly frustrated. Aroused frustration may dispose the child to behave in ways which interact with dispositional and situational variables. Experiments have been carried out studying the effects of frustration in children on the tendency to remember aggressive or nonaggressive materials presented on film. The results are somewhat equivocal. One study found that frustrated children remember more aggressive material than nonfrustrated children, but a follow-up study did not obtain this effect (Maccoby, Levin, and Selya, 1955, 1956). In a later study by the same senior experimenter, designed to study related issues, boys remembered more aggressive content when the agent of aggression in the film was a boy. The results suggest that identification played a significant role in recall (Maccoby and Wilson, 1957). From these studies it is hard to make predictions about overt behavior. Learning (memory) was studied, not performance of aggressive acts. The results suggest that boys may learn about aggressive behavior from violent TV heroes with whom they may identify. Clearly some boys act out such learning by playing cops and robbers and cowboys and Indians. Whether such knowledge is often used in encounters which lead to injury of others is unclear and not deducible from the studies cited.

Experiments often suffer from a failure to observe directly human aggressive behavior. For instance, some studies rely on inferences drawn from responses to projective psychological tests. The relationship between responses to projective tests and overt behavior in daily life, however, is obscure. For instance, attempts to predict the child's overt aggressive behavior from projectives such as the Thematic Apperception Test depend upon knowledge of inhibitory factors which can sometimes be inferred from knowledge of parents' social class or parents' punitiveness of aggression. The findings of studies where projective tests are administered after exposure to various films depicting violence provide little evidence that exposure either facilitates or reduces overt aggression (Albert, 1957; Emery, 1959).

An intriguing series of experiments have clearly demonstrated the ability of nursery school children to learn novel combinations of behavior by observation. Children are able to remember and later reproduce some sequences of behavior if they watch a person performing that sequence or if they view it on film or in cartoon form. Observation, given some degree of arousal and attention, seems to be sufficient to allow the three-, four-, or five-year-old child to approximately match certain verbal and nonverbal chains of action (Bandura and Walters, 1963).

The group carrying out these experiments has made a clear distinction between observational learning and actual performance. Learning is seen to be under the influence of perceptual contiguity, that is, one has only to observe stimulus events following each other in order to learn. Performance, however, is considered to be chiefly influenced by reinforcement, by the consequences of overtly producing what was observed. A child may learn by observation and then imitate what he has seen. Whether he imitates again is said to depend on whether his actions lead to reward (positive reinforcement), punishment (negative reinforcement), or no consequences (lack of reinforcement). Positive consequences tend to increase the frequency of any specific imitative behavior, negative reinforcement to suppress it, and no reinforcement to eliminate or extinguish it (Bandura and Walters, 1963).

Most of the experiments on observational learning and imitation follow a basic paradigm. Individual children are exposed to (allowed to observe) a model (film or cartoon characters are sometimes used) who engages in distinctive aggressive verbal statements and who plays aggressively with toys in a room. The children are then left alone, one at a time, in a room full of aggressive and non-aggressive toys, and their verbal and nonverbal behavior is recorded. The principal measure is the degree to which they imitate the aggressive acts and verbalizations of the person they observed. The behavior of the exposed children is compared both to the behavior of the model and to the behavior of other children who observed a model who did not speak or act aggressively (Bandura and Huston, 1961; Bandura, Ross, and Ross, 1961, 1963a, 1963b).

The studies demonstrate that children imitate the specific aggressive verbalizations and actions of the model. They also tend to play more aggressively in general if they observe an aggressive model than if the model is nonaggressive. Imitation has further been shown to be greater if the model is rewarded (vicarious reinforcement) or if the children are promised rewards, after exposure, for reproducing the behavior of the model. Children imitate, but considerably less, if the model is punished or is not rewarded. A number of parameters of imitation have been explored. Boys are more likely to imitate the aggressive talk and play of a man than of a woman. Children are more likely to imitate a nurturant person than a person who does not interact with them. Dependent, low self-esteem children previously rewarded for imitation are more likely to imitate than children who are independent, have high self-esteem, or are not used to being rewarded for imitation (Bandura and Walters, 1963).

Several problems arise in any attempt to extrapolate the results of this series of experiments to the possible naturalistic behavioral effects of viewing televised fantasy violence. First, no aggression occurs in these studies in the sense of injury to person or property. The model from whom the children learn by observation verbally and physically aggresses toward, for example, a large inflated plastic doll and not toward another person. This action may be termed aggressive play, but there is no destructive consequence. Second, the imitative aggression of the child can have no adverse consequences for others or himself. He is alone and his imitation and other activities are limited to verbalizations and play with toys. Although these studies raise the clear possibility that children may learn aggressive techniques (how to hit with a mallet or how to call names) by watching audiovisual displays, little information is conveyed concerning the probability that such learning will be performed when it will have important consequences for the child or others.

One may assume that any imitative performance influenced by the media is regulated by already existing inhibitions as well as by expected or actual consequences of overt acts. Furthermore, the experimental situations maximized in many ways the probability of imitation. The child was placed in the same situation with the same objects he had just observed. The child remained alone with the same objects in the same room immediately after observing, with no distractions, while being allowed to feel that no one was watching. Seldom, if ever, does this convenient set of circumstances occur for the child viewing television. There are distractions, often others are present, and a toy machine gun, rubber knife, or other aggressive toy may not be available for imitative purposes. Nevertheless, the proposition that children may under certain circumstances behave aggressively in a manner observed on television or films must be taken seriously.

Experiments related to the possible effects which television viewing may have on behavior have almost all utilized either children of preschool age (nursery or kindergarten) or college sophomores taking introductory psychology courses. This peculiar choice of ages seems to be dictated not by theoretical considerations or the importance of understanding the phenomena at these ages, but by the availability of subjects. Most universities and colleges have a nursery school in the vicinity, and the young children there are usually available for a worthwhile study since they are not busy with reading, writing, or arithmetic. Once the child enters the first grade, schools become somewhat reluctant to let him spend time in experiments. The college sophomore taking introductory psychology often serves in experiments as a requirement for completing the course. This availability has led to an unfortunate state of affairs. Certain classes of people are studied because they can be studied readily and not because they necessarily should be. The behavior of children or adults of other ages about whom we should know much more remains a relative mystery. Age is not the only issue; both the nursery school child at the university-connected school and the college sophomore tend to be white, middle class, and of considerably above average intelligence. Findings from these select groups may not be applicable to the majority of the population. Much of our knowledge of behavior is based on the white rat, the rhesus monkey, the university-connected nursery school child, and the college student, and although this progression is phylogenetically and ontogenetically valid, it leaves some rather large gaps to be filled. Fortunately some psychologists interested in developmental and educational psychology have begun to fill these gaps (Singer and Singer, 1969).

Experiments have been conducted, utilizing college students, on the effects of exposure to violent motion picture materials on the subjects' levels of hostility. In a typical design angered (by being insulted) or nonangered subjects were either exposed or not exposed to a part of a movie showing a violent fight (boxing) sequence (Feshbach, 1961). The findings indicated that if college students are first angered by being insulted, their level of hostility after insult is lowered by being allowed to watch the brutal boxing scenes. There seemed to be no effect on the level of hostility shown by nonangered subjects. There were no measures of the tendency to overtly injure anyone or to damage real property; rather, questionnaires and word association tests were used to measure the students' levels of hostility. Extrapolations to possible overt behavior would be relatively speculative.

Two possible explanations of the above results have been proposed. The first is the drive reduction, or catharsis, explanation. The angered subjects are posited to have a high level of aggressive drive which is partially lowered by perceiving a violent fantasy sequence on film. The viewers experience some degree of drive reduction by watching someone get badly hurt in the film sequence. The resultant lowering of aggressive drive is considered to be reinforcing. The second explanation involves an inhibition effect. This viewpont assumes that the angered subjects seeing the brutal fight sequence engage in fantasies concerning how they would like to hurt someone badly, chiefly the person who insulted them. These fantasies in turn

are frightening; they arouse anxiety and guilt about hurting someone and about possible retaliation. Affected by the aroused guilt and
anxiety, the angered subjects are said to inhibit their hostile thoughts
and feelings. Consequently their level of hostility is lowered (Berkowitz, 1964). Some evidence supports the catharsis hypothesis although it is certainly not proven yet. However, whatever the mechanisms involved, if people are operating under high aggressive
arousal, exposure to hostile fantasy material may lower hostile
thought and feelings. However, considerable qualifying and conflicting evidence must be taken into account. For instance, the
subjects' states of hostility will be affected by the content of the
films they view. If there is a villain and he is physically punished
in the film, angered subjects express more hostility toward the person who insulted them than if a nonvillain is injured. Furthermore,
if a film shows a bad guy being physically punished, the viewers
are likely to deliver overt punishment to a person who is also considered to be bad. Clearly, mere exposure to violent fantasy materials
does not guarantee a catharsis effect (Berkowitz, 1962; Berkowitz,
Corwin, and Hieronimus, 1963; Berkowitz and Rawlings, 1963).

Such studies have several limitations when they are utilized
to make assumptions about the effects which the viewing of violent
fantasy programs on television have on people in naturalistic settings. First, few studies have used measures of overt aggression.
Most have utilized indices of hostility or aggressive drive inferred
from projective or paper and pencil tests of attitudes, feelings, preferences, or associative thought. Furthermore, single filmed sequences
or several still pictorial presentations have been used with little of
the variety and complexity of content of which repeated television
exposure consists. In some programs both the hero and the villain
get hurt to different extents for different reasons; the effect on the
viewer may vary with the degree of injury, the reason for the injury,
and whether the viewer sympathizes with the victim.

In one of the better controlled experimental studies, in which
increments in aggression following exposure to film violence were
found in both experimentally angered and control delinquent subjects, a two-minute film was employed as the stimulus (Hartmann,
1969). Inasmuch as only the second minute of that film consisted of

aggressive interaction, the observers did not have much opportunity to identify with heroes, work through feelings, or bring cognitive mechanisms into play. In any case, a very short sequence may be qualitatively as well as quantitatively different from a television drama. Walters and his collaborators, however, have effectively demonstrated that exposure to aggressive film content can affect social interaction as well as individual play activities. In a series of experiments using hospital attendants, high school boys, and young women from a hotel for working girls, experimental subjects witnessed an aggressive scene from the motion picture *Rebel Without a Cause* while control subjects watched a film of adolescents cooperating in constructive activities. The dependent measure, administered before and after the film exposure, consisted of the subject's administering electric shock in a fictitious learning experiment to a confederate of the experimenter. All three experimental groups showed a significantly greater increase in the shock levels used than did their respective controls. In addition, the experimental males scored higher than the control males on the Buss-Durkee inventory of aggression. The difference for girls was insignificant. The results obtained are particularly impressive in view of the replication and the direct, interpersonal character of the dependent measure of aggression (Walters, Thomas, and Archer, 1962; Walters and Thomas, 1963).

Recent experimentation indicates that the presentation or presence of weapons such as a gun may increase the willingness of college subjects to inflict injury on others (Berkowitz and Buck, 1967). In actuality the students in the experiment are not hurting anyone; however, they think they are. Willingness to deliver electric shocks to another person increases if an object with possible violent functions, such as a gun, is placed in the experimental room where the subjects can perceive it. Again, tempting though it may be, it is not safe to assume that viewing a gun on television might cause a child to hurt someone. The very fact than an experimenter allows a student in a college laboratory to use an apparatus which he is told will deliver shocks to a fellow student sets up a permissive rather than an inhibitory setting for aggression. Furthermore, it is hard to tell what the student guesses or speculates about a gun's being introduced and how it should affect his delivery of electric shocks. Certainly restraints or inhibitions against aggression are absent. Nevertheless, the experimental results raise the very real possibility that actual or pictorial presentation of objects associated with violence may increase violent behavior.

Other somewhat similar pertinent studies have been carried out with equivalent limitations (Berkowitz and Holmes, 1960). Permission to give electric shocks is given by the experimenter. Shock is in fact demanded, although the subject can decide how many shocks to give and how intense the shock will be. (In actuality no shock is given, and subjects are told this when their part in the study is concluded.) Certainly the child in daily life is seldom given permission to decide how much to hurt someone right after he has seen a television program involving aggression. Many studies separate the person doing the shocking from the injured party so that the aggressor cannot discover what the consequences of his act are. In addition, there are usually no consequences for the aggressor contingent on the aggressive act; that is, reprisal is not possible or feared. The child or young adult at home or at a friend's house, however, is in a situation where hurting someone else has often had very real consequences.

Our survey of the pertinent research leads to the conclusion that predictions concerning the effects of fantasy violence on aggressive behavior cannot be made with any confidence on the basis of current knowledge. There are few surveys and they do not show clear effects. Generally, they indicate that children expose themselves quite willingly to violence in comics, magazines, books, radio, movies, and television. Disturbed children who suffer severe frustration and who are socially maladept seem to particularly gravitate toward violent television programs and possibly indulge in many aggressive fantasies (Schramm, Lyle, and Parker, 1961).

Clinical psychologists offer opinions ranging from the proposition that comic books and television are major causes of delinquency to the belief that fantasy activities chiefly lower the probability of violent action. Some clinicians and other psychologists chiefly concerned with exploring personality dynamics have a complex view of the function of fantasy in human behavior. They view it chiefly as a coping mechanism and point out that the degree of cognitive development of the child, his ability to test reality and to learn from consequences determine, partly, the functions and effects of fantasy (Singer, 1966). No clinical studies have systematically attempted to ascertain the effects of exposure to hostile fantasy on overt violence. However, clinical work has raised important and vital hypotheses well worth investigating, and extensive work is being done on the general functions of fantasy.

Experimental studies have raised some important issues and findings. Most clear is the fact that children are capable of learning from television and other audiovisual displays of behavior and that they may imitate what they observe under certain circumstances (Bandura and Walters, 1963). Children do not perform everything they learn by observation. The tendency to perform what is observed is determined by a number of variables such as the child's expectations about consequences, opportunities to imitate, previous consequences of behaviors which fall into the same class (such as overt aggression), instigation to perform that class of behaviors, external inhibitions, and conflict with internalized standards.

The findings on the effects of pictorial stimuli of a hostile nature on young adults reveal few significant effects on calm subjects. For whatever reason, there may be a lowering of hostile (aggressive) drive in angry subjects when it is unclear whether the people involved in violence in the film are heroes or villains. When permission to aggress is given by an experimenter who provides the means to hurt others, then the introduction of aggressive pictorial stimuli or actual objects such as guns may facilitate aggressive behavior in the laboratory. Facilitation also occurs if insulted subjects see a "bad" person being punished in a movie. However, none of the experimental studies cited replicate real life viewing and behavioral conditions sufficiently to permit extrapolation to the effects of the depiction of violence in the media on daily behavior.

A concern of some critics of violent fantasy materials is that some children may be adversely affected although the majority are not. Even though there is no significant difference between the two groups, or even if aggressive television fantasy, in general, lowers the probability of overt aggression, how is one to know whether a few children are instigated to behave in a violent fashion by such programs? The hypothesis might be that, for a small minority of children, the nature of their personalities in concert with exposure to a certain program or programs does trigger violent action. It would also be assumed that such occurrences are not frequent enough to be evident in group results. It might be argued further that it is exactly these unusual children, in unusual circumstances, adversely affected by aggressive fantasy materials, who have come to the attention of practicing clinicians who then conclude that violence in mass media is significantly responsible for violence or delinquency.

This issue poses a serious problem for the investigator who attempts to formulate general functional relationships and often does not have the methodological tools to account for what appear to be minor sources of variance. (The finding that aspirins are safe if taken as directed does not ensure that someone cannot have a violent allergic reaction to aspirin.) Nevertheless, this does not mean that such questions are not open to empirical determination. One useful research tactic would be to make a particularly careful study of those subjects who are considered prone to react in the uncommon manner. Another would be to examine those infrequent environmental circumstances which are hypothesized to lead to statistically rare events. Studies may be needed of highly impressionable children and children who are relatively unaffected by inhibitory forces (such as sociopathic or psychopathic children). The effects of televised violence in families where aggression is permitted or even encouraged might be separately studied.

Research findings alone cannot dictate ethical or public policy considerations. Penicillin can be very harmful to a few people even on first administration. For many more people it is the drug that saves their life. Physicians, in general, use penicillin when it is the drug of choice and take the small risk of a possible adverse reaction. One assumes that if an equally useful drug with fewer possible adverse effects existed (or if an allergic reaction were known to be probable), penicillin would not be used. It has been argued that, unlike penicillin, violent television programs have no utility other than the fact that many children and adults like such programs. It may be argued that since there is a great choice of other kinds of programs that people enjoy and since there is some reason to suspect that televised violence may be harmful to some, such violent programs should be banned. Even if there are no large-scale effects, it can be argued that the chance that even a few injuries may be partly caused by watching such shows is enough reason to cancel them.

Others might contend that such an attitude would cause the abolition of swimming, boating, skiing, speed racing, and other sports which can lead to injuries. Children and adults engage in such activities because they like them even though alternative activities are much safer. Certainly deaths of drivers and spectators occasionally result from car races. Whether racing should be abolished, however, is a value judgment. The case for control of violence on television is even more complicated by constitutional issues involving freedom of speech.

If it were demonstrable that televised violence has adverse effects, an issue of public policy would still remain. A decision has to be made whether actual or just suspected undesired effects justify or do not justify the prohibition of certain types of entertainment or behavior. Should people be prevented from smoking or drinking, which are clearly potentially harmful acts? (Drinking may even lead to endangering others.) These are issues on which people can and do differ. For some, censorship is a greater evil than any purported adverse effects of viewing. Research has a bearing on such values and ethical issues. If televised fantasy violence has no demonstrable adverse effects or only infrequent minor ones, the public's wishes and the television industry's actions may be different from what they would be if the effects were major or frequent. Although hopefully influenced by facts produced by careful investigation, decisions must still be based on values and practical considerations. No amount of research can decide whether all the cowboy programs in the world are worth one broken arm or whether one hundred broken arms are equal to the pleasure or other benefits that children may derive from watching the dynamic duo of Batman and Robin in televised action. All one can hope for in a democracy is that an informed public will have an important voice on issues which affect their lives. However,

to be informed means to be in possession of facts rather than un-
founded opinions. Part of the task of social scientists is to produce
the facts.

The question of the effects of viewing aggressive content on
TV is very much an open one. On the one hand, there are survey
data on the basis of which it is difficult to establish functional relationships and, on the other hand, there are laboratory studies with
reasonably clear causal interpretations, based on small samples,
whose applicability to naturalistic TV exposure and real effects are
questionable. What appeared to be required was an experimental
study involving prolonged and intensive viewing of aggressive and
nonaggressive TV content and measurement of effects on overt
aggressive behaviors such as fighting and swearing and on mediating cognitive structure and covert behaviors such as aggressive
attitudes, preferences, and fantasies. It also appeared desirable to
take into account individual differences in aggressive drive, overt
aggressive expression, emotional control, and related personality and
demographic variables which might contribute to or modify the
influence of TV exposure.

In order to gain control over the total TV viewing activities
of the boys, it was decided that only boys living in a preparatory
school, military academy, or other school or home for boys would be
utilized in the study. In this way, the staff of the institutions and the
experimenters would have complete control over how much and
what type of TV viewing would be engaged in by each boy. In
addition, the residential settings would greatly facilitate the recording of the boys' behavior, especially in regard to aggressive incidents.
Altogether, seven schools and institutions, five in the greater Los
Angeles area and two in the greater New York area, participated in
the research project. A public high school and junior high school
were also used to provide a comparison population against which to
test the normality of the test responses of the residential school population.

The formulation and testing of explicit experimental hypotheses, while desirable, was secondary to the main purpose of this
investigation. Our primary objective was to determine the effects
of sustained exposure to predominantly aggressive or nonaggressive

television content on aggressive values and behaviors. A number of processes mediate the influence of television exposure upon an audience. The outcome of television exposure depends on the strength of various parametric variables and the resolution of the partly conflicting processes to which these variables are related. We were able to estimate the strength of some of these variables through our measuring procedures but could not hope to assess all pertinent factors. Consequently, we focused our analysis on evaluation of the experimental effects, investigating these effects as functions of variables which, on the basis of prior empirical studies, theoretical considerations, and social interest, we considered relevant.

We did entertain a number of secondary hypotheses that posit a complex interaction between the experimental treatment, personality variables, and the nature of the aggressive response. While we now would not conceptualize the problem in quite the same manner, and although only a relatively small portion of the statistical analysis bears upon these hypotheses, they are nevertheless of theoretical interest. One of these hypotheses was that children high in both overt aggression and covert aggression will show a cathartic effect and will show significantly less direct aggression and less fantasy hostility and related effects after long term exposure to aggressive TV content than after similar exposure to nonaggressive TV content. A second hypothesis was that children low in both overt aggression and covert aggression will experience disinhibiting and arousing effects and will show a rise in covert hostile fantasy and related variables and, possibly, a rise in some aspects of overt aggression after exposure to nonaggressive TV content. The third hypothesis was that children high in covert aggression and low in overt aggression will show a significant decrement in fantasy aggression and a significant increment in direct aggression after exposure to aggressive TV content as compared with similar exposure to nonaggressive TV content.

These hypotheses are based on the following assumptions and arguments: First, high covert aggression is indicative of strong aggressive drive while low covert aggression is more ambiguous and may indicate either weak drive or strong inhibition. Second, high covert, low overt aggressive children are relatively high in aggression anxiety while children who are high in both forms of aggression are relatively low in aggression anxiety. Third, covert aggression is a more sensitive indicator of aggressive drive than is overt aggression, whereas the latter is relatively more influenced by aggression anxiety and is probably a better index of the strength of the predisposition to respond with instrumental aggression. Fourth, displaced aggression, particularly where it takes a socially approved form, is a positive function of inhibition as well as of aggressive drive and aggressive habits. Fifth, exposure to aggressive TV content tends to reduce the level of aggressive drive and aggression anxiety of high covert, low overt aggressive children and, at the same time, tends to reinforce aggressive acts. Sixth, changes in aggression in children who are initially high in overt as well as covert aggression reflect primarily the cathartic effects of sustained exposure to aggressive TV content since these children already freely express aggression. And, seventh, in the case of children who are initially low in covert and overt aggression, there is minimal opportunity for drive reduction to take place and the stimulating and reinforcing consequences of exposure to aggressive TV content are paramount.

THREE

The Subjects
and the Experiment

All research involves a series of choices among a number of options, each of which has positive and negative components. In deciding on some empirical procedure, one typically relinquishes one desirable feature in order to maximize another. The researcher rarely has ideal options available to him; the present study is no exception. Ideally, we would have carried out this study with random samples of children drawn from different socioeconomic, racial, and geographic areas. Apart from constraints imposed by limited funds, we were also constrained by the need to provide a reasonable degree of control over television exposure for an ex-

49

tended period of time. It would have been exceedingly difficult to regulate television viewing in individual households, where several individuals besides the particular child participating in our study might require access to the television set. In addition, it would have been difficult to maintain adequate checks on the television viewing behavior of the participant child. Still another consideration influencing our choice of population and our overall approach was the desire to obtain measures of aggressive actions. While we could interview or administer questionnaire measures to children and their parents who were sampled from individual households, we could not obtain direct measures of their aggressive activity in the household and in the neighborhood. With sufficient cooperation from the children and the schools they attended, we could, however, obtain useful measures of aggressive behaviors that occurred in the school situation.

Given the need for obtaining certain kinds of data and, most importantly, exercising adequate control over our major independent variable—type of television program observed—we chose to carry out the study in institutional settings. The problem, of course, in utilizing institutional settings is the special nature of the populations and the difficulty of generalizing from these samples to the normative child. We recognized that no matter how we chose the institutional samples, the children and the viewing situation would differ in some respects from the typical child in a typical home. To minimize this difference, we avoided institutions with markedly deviant populations and restricted our study to private academies and residences for boys with inadequate home care facilities or with minor social adjustment problems.

The experimental sample was limited to boys although it would have been desirable to include girls as well. Since our resources were limited, we decided to focus on the population whose aggressive behavior is a matter of social concern. While girls can certainly be aggressive, physically aggressive acts are largely the province of boys. Also, since we wished to examine the impact of aggressive and nonaggressive television on different personality subgroups, it was desirable to have a large sample of at least one sex, to ensure sufficient numbers in each personality grouping. Of greater concern than the restriction to one sex is the age restriction of the sample. The preschool child and the primary grade child are not included in the study. Too few of these children are in institutional settings. In addition, it was desirable, although not critical, to use the same measuring instruments for all populations. We could not have administered our questionnaires to younger children. Our findings cannot be and should not be generalized to younger children. Another experimental study, utilizing a somewhat different approach, should be carried out with a younger population.

Necessity rather than desirability also resulted in the restriction of the geographical areas in which the participating institutions were located to Southern California and New York City. It was important that the institutions be located reasonably close to the investigators (Professor Singer was on the staff of New York University at the time), to permit adequate implementation and supervision of a rather complex experimental field study. Seven residential schools and institutions, five in Southern California and two in the greater New York area, participated in the project. The California group consisted of three private schools—the Cate School, the Ojai Valley School, and the Army and Navy Academy—and two boys' homes—the McKinley Home for Boys and the Pacific Lodge Boys' Home. The New York institutions were both Catholic homes for boys—St. Vincent's Home and St. John's Home. Both the Cate School and the Army and Navy Academy are boys' schools. The Ojai Valley School is coeducational and, primarily for administrative reasons, a small number of girls were included in the experiment conducted at the school.

The three private schools all provide college preparatory programs, charge similar sums for tuition and residence, and draw their children from primarily upper middle class homes. The Cate School offers a four-year high school curriculum while the Army and Navy Academy and Ojai Valley have junior high divisions. The latter also has an elementary program with the age range descending to eight. The atmosphere, goals, and population of the Cate School are very similar to those of the better New England prep schools. The Ojai Valley students are somewhat more heterogeneous in ability, and the atmosphere at the school tends to be more informal.

The population of the Army and Navy Academy is still more heterogeneous than that of Ojai; the Academy, as a military school, presents a different atmosphere from Cate and Ojai. The Pacific Lodge Boys' Home is a charitable institution and is supported by the Los Angeles United Way and various child placement agencies. Like each of the other boys' homes, it provides general supervision, treatment, and guidance to boys. Pacific Lodge focuses on adolescents; age at entrance is usually thirteen to fifteen, the boy being placed for reasons of social and personal adjustment difficulties or lack of adequate home care. The McKinley Home provides residential care and treatment for boys between eight and eighteen. It accepts placements from parents and guardians as well as from social agencies and has special fee arrangements with the former group. The children from both homes attend local public schools. St. Vincent's Home for Boys and St. John's Home for boys have similar age populations, except that the average age of the St. John's boys is younger, ranging within the junior high or high school level, while St. Vincent's has a number of high school age boys. Both institutions are run by the Archdiocese of Brooklyn and, like McKinley and Pacific Lodge, are for boys whose families are unable or unfit to take care of them. Boys are placed not on the basis of personal problems but solely on the grounds of lack of proper home care. About 35 per cent of the children in the boys' homes are black and an additional 10 per cent are of Spanish-speaking backgrounds. The residents of the private schools are predominantly white and from upper middle class backgrounds.

The size of the experimental sample was subject to considerable fluctuation. There were 625 participants randomly assigned to the aggressive or control (nonaggressive) TV viewing groups; for these boys behavior observations are available. The number who took the premeasures and whose forms were legible was 511. This difference is due largely to the fact that 121 boys from the Army and Navy Academy were not present at the pretest because of illness, but they participated in the TV viewing. As Table 1 indicates, the number is still lower for the posttest and drops to 395 for the pre-post change measures. Differential absences on the pretest and posttest, unsigned questionnaires and ones difficult to match, and some withdrawal from the experiment during the last few weeks were the major reasons for the smaller number available for the pre-post change comparisons. Table 1 lists the numbers for the participating institutions.

The experimental procedures and objectives were reviewed in detail with the headmasters and directors of the participating institutions. At the Army and Navy Academy and St. Vincent's Home participation by the boys was compulsory. In the other five institutions the boys volunteered for the project. The boys and the cottage supervisors and teachers who were to record and rate their behavior were told that the study concerned the relationship between the evaluation of different types of TV programs and the personality and attitudes of the viewer. They were further told that they would be assigned to a specific set of programs and that one of the conditions for participation in the experiment was that they stick to the specified set of programs. The reasons given for assigning individuals to particular program groups were twofold: First, it would ensure continuity in the viewing and that we could get some information based on repeated viewing of the same program or same type of program; second, we would get better evaluations of a particular program if the viewers were familiar with similar programs. Most of the boys and the supervisors appeared to accept these explanations. Intensive interviewing of a sample of participants following completion of the experiment indicated that while several felt that the object of the project was to study the influence on children of exposure to aggression on television, a substantial majority accepted the explanation of the experimenters or else entertained some other hypothesis irrelevant to the main purpose of the study.

Two procedures were used for assignment of subjects to the aggressive or control (nonaggressive) TV diets. At Ojai, Cate, and the Army and Navy Academy, the boys were randomly assigned to an aggressive or control treatment on an individual basis. The TV programs were viewed in classrooms and, in a few instances, in faculty homes. The boys' dormitory and room arrangements at these schools did not permit adequate centralized control in their dwelling areas. At the various boys' homes, where the children were clustered in cottages or on floors with supervisors living with them, it was best

Table 1. NUMBER OF SUBJECTS BY INSTITUTION

		A	B	C	D	E	F	G	Total
					INSTITUTIONS				
S's participating (behavior observations available)	Control	18	46	26	113	36	50	20	309
	Agg. TV	18	36	23	118	35	62	24	316
	Total	36	82	49	231	71	112	44	625
N available for premeasures after absences and exclusion of illegible forms.	Control	18	43	23	73	36	50	18	261
	Agg. TV	18	33	22	67	33	53	24	250
	Total	36	76	45	140	69	103	42	511
N available for postmeasures after absences and exclusion of illegible forms.	Control	1	39	26	83	36	50	18	253
	Agg. TV	7	24	22	81	32	54	23	243
	Total	8	63	48	164	68	104	41	496
N available for prepost change questionnaire measures.	Control	1	37	23	48	36	42	16	203
	Agg. TV	7	23	21	38	31	49	23	192
	Total	8	60	44	86	67	91	39	395

A: Cate
B: McKinley
C: Pacific Lodge
D: Army and Navy
E: Ojai
F: St. Vincent's
G: St. John's

to locate the TV sets in the dwelling units. At McKinley, individual cottages, paired by age, were randomly assigned to the two experimental treatments. At Pacific Lodge, random assignment of both individuals and clusters of boys was utilized. Half a dwelling unit was assigned to the aggressive and half to the control treatment. At St. Vincent's and St. John's, the boys on one end of a floor were assigned to one treatment condition and those at the other end were assigned to the other treatment. The size of the viewing groups at the different settings varied from ten to eighteen.

The boys were required to watch a minimum of six hours of television a week for six weeks. At St. Vincent's and St. John's there were two-hour viewing periods, seven days a week, so the minimum was greatly exceeded. The participants could view as much television as they wanted, provided they watched programs from the designated list. After each program the boys individually indicated the degree to which they liked the program and the affects it elicited on a program rating form provided them. At St. John's and St. Vincent's, they were required to complete a form for only one program a day rather than for each program seen.

At three of the institutions, monitors or captains were appointed from among the boys to help the cottage mother, staff counselor, or teacher collect the forms and regulate the TV viewing. To encourage the cooperation of the boys and to help make the experiment a positive experience for them, they were each promised and given ten dollars for completing the six-week viewing period. This was not done at the Army and Navy Academy and probably should have been, in view of the number of boys at that school who managed not to take the pre- and posttests. Every effort was made to reduce possible sources of frustration associated with the experiment. Thus, boys were permitted to drop out if they wished (even where participation was initially compulsory), since it was felt that resentment induced by forced compliance might override any experimental effect. When a number of boys in the control group at three of the institutions objected very strongly because "Batman" was not on their list, they were permitted to watch "Batman." We were very conscious of the fact that, on the whole, the aggressive diet was more attractive to the boys and we tried to minimize any frustration associated with being assigned to the control diet.

The current TV programs that appeared during the evening and weekend hours during which television was available to the boys were categorized as aggressive or nonaggressive by three raters. Differences between raters occurred infrequently, the percentage of agreement between pairs of raters varying from 90 to 96 per cent. Programs which depicted fighting, shooting, and other forms of physical violence were considered aggressive. These included cowboy, spy, detective, police, and war themes. The aggressive diet is listed in Table 2 and the nonaggressive diet in Table 3. Many more nonaggressive than aggressive programs were available.

A number of personality tests and attitude scales were administered at the beginning and end of the six-week experimental period. In addition, daily behavior rating forms were completed for each child for the experimental period and, in most instances, during the week before and the week after the six-week TV viewing period.

The behavior rating scale (Appendix Form A) consisted of twenty-six items, nineteen of which related to aggressive acts. Rating and recording these aggressive acts were the responsibility of the house parent, supervisor, teacher, or proctor most familiar with the daily activities of the boy to be rated. A rating sheet was completed for each boy five days a week for the duration of the experiment. In the California schools, the ratings were initiated four to seven days before the study began, and in both California and New York they continued for a week after the experiment was over. Each aggressive act was rated as provoked or unprovoked and mild or moderate-strong. If the behavior was provoked and mild, it was given a weight of 1; if provoked and moderate, a weight of 2; if unprovoked and mild, a weight of 3; and if unprovoked and moderate or strong, a weight of 4. The total score on the nineteen aggressive items could range from 0 to 76. The sum of the weighted scores for the daily rating schedule constituted the child's aggressive behavior score on each date. Separate scores were derived for aggression directed toward peers and aggression directed toward authority. The behavior rating scale was pretested on boys at the Fernald School at UCLA and, on the basis of the pretest, was revised. A reliability

Table 2. AGGRESSIVE TV PROGRAMS

Alfred Hitchcock Presents
Arrest and Trial
Baron
Bat Masterson
Batman
Battle Cry
Big Valley
Blue Angels
Blue Light
Bonanza*
Branded*
Chained
Chiller
Colt 45*
Combat*
Dagora, Space Monster
Daktari
Danger Is My Business
Daniel Boone
Death Valley Days
Detectives
FBI*
Foreign Intrigue
Fugitive
Get Smart
Gigantor
Gunsmoke*
Have Gun, Will Travel*
Hercules
High and Wild
Highway Adventure
Honey West*
I Spy*
Jet Attack
Laredo*
Law and Mr. Jones
Legend of Jesse James*

Loner
Man Called Shenandoah*
Man from Uncle
Manhunt
Marshal Dillon*
Maverick
Mongols
Mummy
Outer Limits*
Perry Mason
Rebel
Rifleman*
Rogues
Route 66*
Roy Rogers
Run for Your Life
Sea Chase
Sea Hunt
Secret Agent
77 Sunset Strip
Sky King
Space Robinson
Steel Helmet
Superman
Tarzan
Thief of Bagdad
Trials of O'Brien
Twelve O'Clock High*
Twilight Zone
Untouchables*
Virginian*
Voyage to the Bottom of the Sea
Wild, Wild West*
Wrestling
Wyatt Earp
Zorro*

*Starred programs constitute the basic diet while the nonstarred programs were supplementary and were seen less frequently.

Table 3. Nonaggressive TV Programs

Adventure
Alumni Fun
Amateur Hour*
America
American Bandstand*
Andy Griffith
Andy Williams*
Ann Sothern
Art of Films
Bachelor Father*
Batman^a
Bell Telephone Hour*
Beverly Hillbillies*
Bewitched*
Big Show
Big Valley
Billy Barty
Bobby Lord Show
Cal's Corral
Camp Runamuck*
Candid Camera
Carol +2
CBS Sports Spectacular
Cinderella
Clay Cole Diskotec
College Basketball
College Report
Concern
Dance Time
Danny Kaye*
Daughters of Orange
Dean Martin
Dialing for Dollars
Dick Van Dyke Show*
Discovery 66
Dobie Gillis
Doctor Kildare
Donna Reed*
Ed Sullivan*

Existence
Expedition
Face the Nation
Faces and Places
Farmer's Daughter*
Flintstones*
Flipper
Folk Guitar
Gadabout Gaddis*
GE College Bowl*
Gemini 8
Gene Davis Show
Gidget*
Gilligan's Island*
Golden Voyage*
Gomer Pyle*
Grand Ole Opry*
Green Acres*
Hank*
Happy Wanderer*
Hazel*
High Adventure
Holiday
Hollywood and the Stars
Hollywood Backstage
Hollywood Palace
Huckleberry Hound
Hullabaloo*
I Dream of Jeannie
Islands of Paradise
Islands in the Sun
I've Got a Secret
Jackie Gleason
Jimmie Dean Show
Joan Davis Show
John Forsythe Show*
Jubilee Tonight
Judge Bean
Lassie*

^a Batman, although considered an aggressive program, was included in both diets.

Table 3.   NONAGGRESSIVE TV PROGRAMS (cont.)

Lawrence Welk*

Leave it to Beaver*

Life of Riley

Linkletter's Hollywood Talent
  Scouts

Lloyd Thaxton

Lost in Space

Lucy Show

McHale's Navy*

McKeever and the Colonel

Meet Me in Las Vegas

Meet the Press

Melody Ranch*

Merv Griffin

Michelangelo

Mister Ed*

Mona McCluskey*

Movie Musical

Mr. Roberts*

Murray the K

My Favorite Martian*

My Friend Flicka*

My Mother, the Car*

My Three Sons*

Museum Open House

NBC Sports in Action

NY Talent Search

Of Lands and Seas

Opinion in the Capitol

Our Miss Brooks

Ozzie and Harriet*

Passport to Travel

Patti Duke*

People's Choice

Petition

Petticoat Junction*

Peyton Place

Please Don't Eat the Daisies*

Polka Parade*

Red Skelton*

Rendezvous with Adventure

Request for Performance

Roving Kind*

Sammy Davis Show

Scholar Quiz

Science in Action

Shebang

Shindig*

Shivaree*

Ski Breed

Ski Scene

Ski Spree

Smothers Brothers*

Something Special

Sports

Step This Way

Surfing World

Surf's Up

Tammy*

Teacher 66*

This Exciting World

To Tell the Truth*

Top 40

Viewpoint

Walt Disney's Wonderful World
  of Color*

Wanderlust*

Wide World of Sports*

Wild Kingdom

Winchell Mahoney Show

Wonderful World of Golf

Wonders of the World*

Woody Woodpecker

Yogi Bear

You Asked for It

Zoorama

*Starred programs constitute the basic diet while the nonstarred
programs were supplementary and were seen less frequently.

study conducted between two raters who, on a specific date, had differential degrees of contact with a group of fifteen boys reflected a high correlation between the raters in their rank ordering of boys although there was less agreement in the individual aggression rating scores recorded for each child. This latter difference was to be expected inasmuch as one rater was the classroom teacher while the second was a teaching supervisor who observed the class for various periods during the day.

The personality inventory contained seventy-nine items which yielded five trait measures. The Minnesota Multiphasic Personality Inventory (MMPI) Lie Scale was also included in the inventory. The five scales were taken from different sources. In each case a score of 0 or 1 was assigned to each item in the scale, and the sum of these scores constituted the total score on that scale. The first and second trait measures, the overt hostility scale consisting of ten items and the covert hostility scale consisting of fourteen items, were based on Bendig's (1962) revision of the Buss-Durkee Inventory. The overt hostility scale contained manifest aggressive items, for example, "When I really lose my temper, I might slap someone," while the covert hostility items reflected anger, resentment, and suspiciousness, for example, "Although I don't show it, I am sometimes eaten up with jealousy." The third trait measure, the neurotic undercontrol scale, was developed by Jack Block and was based on a factor analytic study of MMPI and California Personality Inventory (CPI) items. There were nineteen items in this scale, which reflected impulsiveness, lack of future goal orientation, and self-centeredness, for example, "I must admit I often try to get my own way regardless of what others may want."

The fourth trait measure, the conflict scale, was developed by Saltz and Epstein (1963) and reflected disturbance over hostile feelings and behavior. The scale consisted of eight items, for example, "I wish I could find a way to handle my angry feelings more satisfactorily." The fifth trait measure, the aggression anxiety measure, was developed by the senior author in connection with another research project. It consisted of nineteen items reflecting ambivalence and anxiety in connection with aggressive feelings and aggressive behavior, for example, "When I get angry, I usually feel bad afterwards," and "It bothers me a lot when I hurt someone else's feelings." Although all the examples cited here were phrased so that agreement with the item contributed to a high score on the scale, each scale included items worded so that disagreement was required for a positive score. Reliabilities reported for these scales have been based largely on college population. These reliability studies have yielded generally satisfactory estimates. The pretest, posttest design of the current project permitted an estimate of the reliabilities of each scale for the age groups in this project. The test-retest reliabilities for each scale for the experimental and for the control groups are reported below.

In the fantasy aggression measure six pictorial stimuli were separately presented by means of a slide projector to groups of the participating boys. Three of the slides were selected from the standard Thematic Apperception Test series—18 GF, 7 BM, and 12M. These respectively depicted a woman often seen as either choking or supporting a second woman, a boy in the foreground with an operation scene in the background, and an older man leaning over a reclining younger man. The remaining three slides were selected from a set specifically designed by Lesser (1958) for the age range employed in the present study. They depicted one boy apparently chasing another, a youngster looking at a second boy with his foot over a book lying on the ground, and a boy holding a ball while a peer has his arm outstretched in a catching position. The boys were asked to make up a story in response to each slide by responding to four questions: What is happening and who are the persons? What has led up to the situation? That is, what has happened in the past? What is being thought and felt and by whom? What will happen?

Codes were established for scoring the degree and type of aggression manifested in the stories and the extent to which anxiety, guilt, or punishment occurred in connection with the expression of aggression. Scoring reliability was established, the agreement between two independent scorers for each of the codes varying from 85 per cent to 95 per cent. The basic measure was the intensity of aggression scale. Scores on this scale could vary from 0 to 3, yielding a range for all six stories of 0 to 18. The criteria used in scoring fantasy stories for intensity of aggression were: when there was no expression of aggression of any kind or intensity in the story, the score was 0. For mild aggression, that is, statements in the story of mild affective states or physical acts which were minor themes or, though part of the major theme, represented nonviolent handling of a provoking situation, for example, irritation, annoyance, disgust, exasperation, self-assertiveness, pushing, and shoving, the score was 1. These were cases of physical aggression with no intent to do bodily harm; they merely expressed mild anger or irritation. Mild accidents and minor illnesses also rated a score of 1. For moderate aggression, that is, statements in the story of strong anger or physical acts integral to the major theme of the story, for example, hate, anger, fury, hitting, jabbing, the score was 2. In these cases physical aggression was undertaken with the expected result of causing the victim pain. Death due to accidents or illness, violent accidents, and violent physical expressions, for example, kicking not specifically intended to inflict pain, also scored 2. For strong aggression, that is, statements about physical acts resulting in death, mutilation, or relatively permanent physical damage or ideas or wishes to the same effect, for example, killing, stabbing, crushing skull, breaking arm, "wish he would die," "think I will kill him," the score was 3.

The aggressive activity preference scale consisted of twelve sets of three activities, for example, "be a musician," "be a private detective," and "be a baseball coach." Each subject was asked to indicate which activity in each set of three he preferred most and which he preferred least. Subjects were told to make single selections in each of these categories even if their preferences seemed equal. One item in each set was considered to be the most aggressive choice for that set, for example, "be a private detective." A measure of preference for aggressive activities was derived as follows: if the item designated most aggressive in a set was checked "most preferred," the subject was given a score of 3 for that set. If the subject checked this item as "least preferred," he was given a score of 0 for that set. If he did not check this item, he was given a score of 1 for the set. The index of aggressive activity preferences was the sum of scores for the twelve sets. Thus, the measure had a possible range of from 0 to 36.

The situation test consisted of six one-sentence descriptions of situations wherein one individual is wronged by another. ("Tom walks out of the room and is tripped by Bill.") Each subject was asked whether each of several possible actions for the offended individual would be right or wrong in that situation. Actions listed ranged from very mild ("ignore it," "ask Bill for an explanation") to verbal aggression ("tell Bill off"), covert aggressive acts ("trip Bill when he gets a chance"), direct physical aggression ("hit Bill a couple of times"), and severe physical aggression ("really beat Bill up"). Each item was assigned a value of 0 to 4 according to severity of the action. Very mild responses were assigned 0, verbal aggression 1, covert aggression 2, direct physical aggression 3, and severe physical aggression 4. A subject's total score consisted of the sum of the item values which he indicated were right. Possible scores ranged from 0 to 54, the highest score being obtained when all aggressive acts were considered right. In addition, the number of times the subject gave each type of response was tabulated separately as an index of style of aggression.

The viewing habits measure listed twelve national television programs, of which six were considered to include aggressive content (for example, "Gunsmoke," "FBI") and six were considered primarily nonaggressive (for example, "My Favorite Martian," "Andy Griffith Show"). The order of the shows was random, but was identical for all subjects. For each show, subjects were asked to indicate their degree of liking for the show and their frequency of watching the show. Subjects were asked to rate all shows for liking, regardless of frequency of watching. Liking for each show was assigned a score ranging from 1 ("dislike it very much") to 5 ("like it very much"); frequency of watching each show was assigned a score ranging from 1 ("have never watched it") to 4 ("watch it regularly"). Four measures were derived: Liking for aggressive shows consisted of the sum of scores on liking for each of the six shows considered to include aggressive content. Scores on this measure thus had a possible range of from 6 to 30. Similarly, liking for nonaggressive shows consisted of the sum of liking scores for the six shows considered primarily nonaggressive. Frequency of watching aggressive shows consisted of the sum of the scores on the frequency scale for the six aggressive shows and could range from 6 to 24. Similarly, frequency of watching nonaggressive shows consisted of the sum of scores on the frequency scale for the six nonaggressive shows.

The case history test gave a brief description of a hypothetical nineteen-year-old's arrest for aggravated assault on an elderly man. The adolescent, named Carl, was described as coming from a badly broken home and having a history of juvenile offenses. Subjects were asked to recommend a prison sentence for Carl on a five-point scale ranging from "suspended sentence" to "more than five years." Longer recommended sentences were considered more aggressive. Subjects were also asked to rate on a five-point scale their degree of agreement or disagreement with each of three statements regarding the treatment of Carl. Two measures were derived: The recommended sentence score consisted of the score on the first item only; thus possible scores on this measure ranged from 1 to 5. The recommended treatment score consisted of the sum of scores on the last three items, a possible range of from 3 to 15.

The aggressive value scale consisted of nineteen statements of opinion relating to aggression. Seven of the items concerned personal aggressive acts, for example, "It is very seldom right to hit another person," while the remaining twelve concerned matters of public policy or generalizations about aggressive behavior, for example, "Teenage hoodlums should be punished severely," "It is the tough guy who always comes out on top." Subjects were asked to rate the degree of their agreement or disagreement with each of the statements on a four-point scale. Higher scores were assigned to agreement with statements favoring aggression and disagreement with statements opposing aggression. Three measures were derived: Aggressive value A consisted of the average score on the seven items concerning personal aggression. Aggressive value B consisted of the average score on the twelve items about public policy and generalizations about aggressive behavior. In addition, each subject's overall average was computed.

The peer rating measure was based on a sociometric rating form developed by Eron and his associates (Eron, 1963). The adaptation employed in this study listed twelve behaviors or characteristics and the names of all the boys in the subject's living group, class, or age group. Nine of the twelve statements referred to aggressive attitudes or acts. Subjects were asked to check which statements applied to each of their peers listed on the form. A score was then derived for each peer. The simplest score derived was the number of aggressive statements checked off for each peer listed. The number of aggressive citations received by a child divided by the number of children rating him constituted the child's aggression rating score.

A program rating form was completed by the subjects immediately after watching each program on their prescribed diet. It required a rating of their degree of liking or disliking for the program on a six-point scale; higher numbers referred to more positive attitudes. Subjects were also asked to indicate the kind and extent of emotional effect the programs had on them. They did this by indicating to what degree they felt good, excited, afraid, bored, annoyed, nervous, angry, sad, happy, and upset. The adjectives were listed with three possible responses: "not at all," "a little," and "very much." The program rating data are extensive; they will not be presented here in detail and are alluded to only insofar as they bear on the interpretation of the major experimental measures.

FOUR

Patterns of
Aggressive Behavior

Of the measures employed in this study, those concerned with overt aggressive behavior are most directly relevant to the social issue of the consequence of exposure to violence on television. The attitudinal, value, and fantasy measures are also important. Changes in the boys' verbal acceptance or rejection of various aggressive behaviors are of interest in their own right and are undoubtedly reflected to some degree in social interaction. Nevertheless, the key pragmatic question is whether or not sustained exposure to the aggressive TV diet produced any measurable effect on the level of aggressive activity. For this reason, the behavior ratings, our best record of actual aggressive acts and incidents, will be analyzed in some detail. Each rater was asked to complete a behavior rating form five times a week for each child in his rating group. In four of the California institutions, the ratings were begun one week before the boys commenced their TV viewing and extended one week beyond the six-week viewing period. In the other institutions the ratings began when the experiment was initiated and, except at one New York school, continued for a week after completion of the experiment.

A first approach to ascertaining differences between the aggressive TV and control groups in aggressive behaviors over the period is simply to compare the average for each group of the total amount of aggression displayed by each child. Difference in peer aggression scores between the control and aggressive TV group is striking and is highly significant statistically. The mean of 151.6 for the controls is almost twice the mean of 81.1 for the aggressive TV group. However, there is a great deal of variation from the mean in the scores of aggressive behavior engaged in by the children and, furthermore, there is more variation among the controls than among the aggressive TV group. (The difference in variation is in itself an interesting finding. It presents a number of statistical problems which we attempted to resolve through several different kinds of analysis.)

There is substantial variation in the number of behavior ratings available for each subject. This variation is in part due to the fact that ratings took place over a period varying from six to eight weeks in the participating institutions. In addition, illness of the rater, illness of the boys, occasional failure by some raters to comply with the experimental instructions, and withdrawal of boys from the study all contributed to the varying number of ratings. In order to reduce the effects of variations in the number of ratings, each boy's aggression score was divided by the number of behavior rating forms submitted for him. This average aggression score is a more descriptive and reliable index and was employed in all subsequent analyses of this key dependent variable. The average aggression scores toward peers and toward authority are reported in Table 4. The differences between the control and the aggressive TV groups remain both substantial and highly significant. The amount of ag-

Table 4.   AVERAGE AGGRESSION[a] TOWARD PEERS AND
TOWARD AUTHORITY

	Peer Aggression		Authority Aggression	
	Aver.	SD	Aver.	SD
Control (N = 309)	2.81	5.0	1.30	1.8
Agg. TV (N = 316)	1.64 p < .01[b]	2.2 p < .01	1.02 p < .03	1.4 p < .01

[a] Based on total aggression scores for each child divided by the number of aggression ratings for that child.
[b] Because of the significant difference in variation, the p value given for the mean difference is based on independent estimates rather than on a pooled estimate of the standard error of the mean difference. This procedure has been followed in all instances where significant differences in variation are present and where parametric tests have been employed.

gression directed toward authority figures was as one might expect, much less than that directed toward peers, and the difference in authority aggression scores between the controls and the aggressive TV groups is much smaller than the corresponding difference in peer aggression. Nonetheless, for both peer and authority aggression, the scores of the control group are reliably higher than those of the aggressive TV group.

The raters themselves were an important source of variation in the aggressive behavior rating scores. One way of reducing the influence of any single rater on the findings is simply to use the rater as a unit of analysis. (This procedure, of course, radically reduces the size of the sample and, as a consequence, provides a highly conservative estimate of the reliability of the difference between the aggressive TV and the control samples.) That more aggressive behaviors toward peers were consistently reported for subjects in the control than in the aggressive TV group is clear from the fact that, in ratings from sixteen of the twenty-two raters who rated both control and aggressive TV subjects, the mean for the control subjects is higher than the mean for the aggressive TV group. (A nonparametric test (Wilcoxin Matched Pairs Signed Ranks) of the difference in peer aggression between the aggressive

TV and control groups, using the twenty-two raters as the sample, yielded a p value at the 5 per cent confidence level. The smaller difference in authority aggression between the experimental and control groups did not attain statistical significance using this method of analysis.) There was also substantial variation among the raters. Since the raters were observing different populations in very different institutional atmospheres, it is difficult, if not impossible, to eliminate this source of variance.

The peer and authority aggression scales represent a summary of specific aggressive acts and communications. The scores on these scales were derived from the frequency with which particular aggressive behaviors toward peer or authority figures were manifested, and from classification of aggressive behaviors as provoked or unprovoked. An unprovoked aggressive act was weighted more heavily than the same act committed in response to provocation. The distinction between provoked and unprovoked is often difficult to make and moreover does not apply with equal cogency to all the behaviors scored. However, theoretical reasons and the fact that the two experimental groups were in contact with each other outside the TV viewing period made it important at least to attempt to distinguish between boys who initiated aggression and boys who responded aggressively.

Table 5 lists the frequency, for each experimental group, of each of the peer-related aggressive behaviors on the behavior rating scale. Since there were approximately the same number of subjects in each experimental condition (311 in the control and 316 in the aggressive TV group), the expected frequencies for each item for the two groups are about the same. The figures under "Total Instances" provide some clues as to which specific behaviors were differentially affected by the experimental treatment. The last two columns of Table 5 indicate the proportion of these behaviors rated as provoked and unprovoked. These data must be interpreted with caution since what has been tabulated are instances of behavior, not number of boys displaying a particular frequency of behavior. Nevertheless, these data indicate which behaviors were affected by the experimental treatment, especially where substantial differences obtain between the experimental and control groups.

Table 5. FREQUENCY OF AGGRESSIVE BEHAVIORS TOWARD PEERS

Items	Group	Total Instances	Proportions	
			Provoked	Unprovoked
1. Fistfight, hitting, kicking	Agg. TV	161	.62	.38
	Control	344	.31	.69
2. Pushing, shoving	Agg. TV	398	.47	.53
	Control	725	.25	.75
3. Angry verbal interchange	Agg. TV	407	.53	.47
	Control	859	.36	.64
4. Cursing	Agg. TV	575	.24	.76
	Control	457	.37	.63
5. Criticizing, insulting	Agg. TV	456	.34	.66
	Control	973	.32	.68
6. Criticism of person not present	Agg. TV	199	.45	.55
	Control	422	.34	.66
7. Grumbling, complaining	Agg. TV	345	.27	.73
	Control	729	.25	.75
8. Rough, destructive with property	Agg. TV	174	.43	.57
	Control	198	.21	.79
13. Bossy	Agg. TV	213	.24	.76
	Control	570	.12	.88

Table 5. FREQUENCY OF AGGRESSIVE BEHAVIORS TOWARD PEERS (cont.)

Items	Group	Total Instances	Proportions	
			Provoked	Unprovoked
14. Bragging, boasting a lot	Agg. TV	246	.20	.80
	Control	515	.12	.88
15. Blaming others	Agg. TV	316	.25	.75
	Control	502	.26	.74
16. Teasing	Agg. TV	516	.31	.69
	Control	834	.18	.82
18. Broke major rule	Agg. TV	111	.29	.71
	Control	145	.24	.76
19. Trying to start trouble	Agg. TV	277	.20	.80
	Control	422	.18	.82
20. Sullen, angry facial expression	Agg. TV	201	.39	.61
	Control	501	.33	.67
21. Seemed jealous	Agg. TV	87	.23	.77
	Control	254	.10	.90
23. Refused tasks	Agg. TV	113	.23	.77
	Control	123	.16	.84
24. Threw object at person	Agg. TV	78	.26	.74
	Control	90	.33	.67
26. Pounded fist, hurt himself	Agg. TV	25	.52	.48
	Control	23	.52	.48

From the item breakdown in Table 5, it can be seen that the greater aggressiveness of the controls was reflected in a variety of aggressive behaviors. There are very sizable differences between the control and aggressive TV groups on physical aggression items, with respect to both the number of instances of such behaviors and the proportion of these aggressive behaviors which were unprovoked. More than twice as many fights occurred among the controls as among the aggressive TV group. Moreover, about two-thirds of the fights in which a control child participated were considered un-provoked whereas less than half the fights in which a boy in the aggressive TV group participated were rated unprovoked. A similar difference, although not quite as striking, holds for the frequencies of pushing and shoving and of rough, destructive handling of prop-erty. The differences between the controls and the aggressive TV group are by no means limited to instances of physical aggression. The control group also displayed much more verbal aggression than did the aggressive TV subjects, particularly as reflected in the abso-lute number and in the relative proportion of unprovoked angry verbal interchanges and teasing. With the exception of two behavior categories which were infrequently scored ("threw object" and "pounded fist") and of cursing, which occurred more often in the aggressive TV group, there was a greater frequency of each aggres-sive behavior in the control sample.

Table 6 lists frequencies of the nonaggressive peer-related items on the behavior rating scale. The differences in these items are much smaller than those in the physical aggression and most of the verbal aggression items. The largest difference is in the item "was picked on," which could be influenced by aggressive behaviors on the part of the child who was picked on. A similar influence could occur on the item "upset when criticized."

On the behavior rating scale of aggressive and nonaggressive behaviors directed toward authority figures, the item differences between the aggressive TV and control groups are not large, except in the category "fistfight, hitting, kicking" which occurred five times as often in the control as in the aggressive TV group. Less aggressive behavior was expressed toward authorities than toward peers. Small differences between experimental and control groups in authority

Table 6. FREQUENCY OF OTHER OBSERVED BEHAVIORS IN INTERACTION WITH PEERS

Items	Group	Total Instances	Proportion Provoked	Proportion Unprovoked
9. Frustrating, unhappy experience	Agg. TV	186	.42	.58
	Control	188	.47	.53
10. Upset when criticized	Agg. TV	231	.35	.65
	Control	313	.24	.76
11. Avoiding people	Agg. TV	298	.23	.77
	Control	385	.34	.66
12. Seemed unhappy	Agg. TV	450	.32	.68
	Control	449	.28	.72
17. Was picked on	Agg. TV	387	.44	.56
	Control	574	.45	.55
22. Especially helpful	Agg. TV	284	.25	.75
	Control	246	.31	.69
25. Overly critical of himself	Agg. TV	76	.37	.63
	Control	53	.24	.76

aggression scores are distributed over the various aggressive behaviors.

Analysis of the experiment sample must take cognizance of the fact that the boys were drawn from very different populations. The seven institutions varied in their ecology and especially in the socioeconomic level and educational orientation of their populations. Although no hypotheses were offered about the possible influence of these variables on the effect of exposure to aggressive content in television, it is likely that marked differences in the type of institution had some bearing on the experimental outcome. These differences may help illuminate the psychological processes mediating the experimental effects. The aggression toward peer scores for controls and aggressive TV boys are presented for each of the seven participating institutions in Table 7. There are statistically significant differences between the aggressive TV and control groups in three of the seven institutions (B, C, F) while in a fourth (G) the difference is significant at the 10 per cent level of confidence. There is an interesting commonality among the four institutions in which a significant effect was obtained which distinguishes them from the three in which there was no reliable experimental effect. Institutions B, C, F, and G are all boys' homes. Their population is primarily working class. The boys are, on the whole, more aggressive than the average adolescent; their IQ's fall in the average and low average range and few boys are college-bound. Institutions A, D, and E are private schools. Their population is predominantly upper middle class. The boys tend to be brighter than average and the great majority plan to go to college. It should also be noted that the participating population in school A was small and that most of the boys did not complete the experiment. There was also a sizable loss in institution D, the military academy.

The breakdown by institutions for aggression toward authority is presented in Table 8. For two institutions (B, G) the mean score of the controls is significantly higher than the corresponding mean for the experimental group. The differences for the remaining two boys' homes and the three private schools are not significant. One would expect a weaker experimental effect on this

Table 7. Average Aggression Toward Peers as a Function of Institution

		INSTITUTION							
		A	B	C	D	E	F	G	Total
Control	Mean	2.93	7.74	4.37	0.55	1.45	4.5ɨ	0.39	2.81
	N	(18)	(46)	(26)	(113)	(36)	(50)	(20)	(309)
Agg. TV	Mean	2.08	3.44	2.55	0.61	1.43	2.74	0.24	1.64
	N	(18)	(36)	(23)	(118)	(35)	(62)	(24)	(316)
		$p > .10$	$p < .01$	$p < .02$	$p > .10$	$p > .10$	$p < .02$	$p = .10$	$p < .001$

Table 8. AVERAGE AGGRESSION TOWARD AUTHORITY AS A FUNCTION OF INSTITUTION

		A	B	C	D	E	F	G	Total
					INSTITUTION				
Control	Mean	1.06	2.16	1.00	0.64	0.88	2.88	0.60	1.30
	N	(18)	(46)	(26)	(113)	(36)	(50)	(20)	(309)
Agg. TV	Mean	0.76	0.97	1.19	0.61	1.16	2.12	0.13	1.02
	N	(18)	(36)	(23)	(118)	(35)	(62)	(24)	(316)
		$p > .10$	$p < .005$	$p > .10$	$p > .10$	$p > .10$	$p > .10$	$p < .001$	$p < .03$

measure since aggression against authority is less well tolerated and meets with more severe sanctions than peer aggression.

It is apparent from these analyses that the experimental differences in aggressive activities hold primarily or only for the boys' homes. They form one population; the middle class, affluent private schools form a second. In subsequent analyses of the behavior ratings, results are separately examined for the private school sample and for the boys' home sample. In addition, a method of statistical analysis has been adopted which is appropriate to the type of data obtained and which also assesses significant trends in aggressive behavior change on a week-by-week basis over the experimental period. This method is a nonparametric analysis of variance procedure, assessing linear trends in each experimental group, differences between linear trends, and overall differences in central tendency.

Before proceeding with the investigation of these changes, a detailed study was made, through factor analytic procedures, of the components of the behavior rating scale. It will be recalled that a previous judgment was made as to which items pertained to aggressive behavior, and only those items that were manifestly aggressive in content were included in the aggressive behavior scores. These a priori judgments were not made in analyzing the components of the scale. As a result a few items which were not included in the previous (general aggression) scale were shown by this empirical analysis to be related to a dimension of aggressive behavior; they therefore appear in the revised scales. The revision resulted in two peer aggression factors and two authority aggression factors. One factor reflects predominantly physical aggression and the other reflects verbal aggression. The verbal aggression and physical aggression toward peers factors are not identical with the corresponding authority aggression factors but there is considerable overlap between verbal aggression toward peers and verbal aggression toward authority and between physical aggression toward peers and physical aggression toward authority. In the subsequent analyses of the behavior rating data, we consider separately the verbal aggression and physical aggression scores for aggression toward peers and aggression toward authority, thereby generating four behavior rating analyses. In addi-

78

tion, the results for the general (non-factor-analyzed) peer aggression scale will be presented for comparative purposes and to provide some continuity with the previously presented data.

The detailed analysis of the behavior ratings was addressed to a number of related questions. First, we were interested in determining the direction and significance of the overall difference on a particular behavioral aggression measure between the control and aggressive TV groups in the boys' home and private school samples. Second, we were interested in assessing whether there was any significant tendency for aggression to increase or decrease over the experimental period. This analysis was made separately for the control and aggressive TV groups. Finally, we wished to establish whether the change in the aggressive TV group was significantly different from the change in the control group. The significance of the difference between the two groups in their change tendencies or linear trends is critical, since an increment or decrement in a particular group is not very revealing. There are many factors other than the experimental treatment which may contribute to change in the behavior aggression scores. What is important is whether the change in one group is reliably different from the change in the other.

These comparisons for the general peer aggression measure are presented in Table 9. There are really two separate tables, one for the boys' homes and the other for the private schools. The first column lists the number of subjects in each group. In the second column are the median general aggression scores for the total experimental period. (The median, while generally comparable to the mean, is less influenced by extreme scores and is the more appropriate descriptive statistic when nonparametric analyses are employed.) It will be noted that, in the case of the boys' homes, the median score for the controls is substantially greater than the median for the aggressive TV group and that this difference between the two groups in aggression toward peers is highly significant. Both boys' home groups have much higher peer aggression scores than either of the private school groups.

The next seven columns indicate the week-by-week median aggression scores; the initial figure (week 1) is the median of the

Table 9. GENERAL AGGRESSION TOWARD PEERS

BOYS' HOMES

	N	Overall Medians	Week-By-Week Medians							Linear Trends
			1	2	3	4	5	6	7	
Control	135	2.98	2.41	1.93	2.00	1.63	2.2	2.94	3.22	+
Agg. TV	138	1.58	1.43	1.18	2.00	.87	1.11	1.30	1.36	—**
p of diff.		<.001	NS							<.04

PRIVATE SCHOOLS

	N	Overall Medians	Week-By-Week Medians							Linear Trends
			1	2	3	4	5	6	7	
Control	160	.51	.39	.48	.15	.39	.42	.17	.18	—*
Agg. TV	167	.47	.09	.19	.32	.26	.19	.17	.17	NS
p of diff.		NS	NS							NS

A ** is used to indicate a linear trend significant at the .01 level, a * for significance at the .05 level and no asterisk for significance at the .10 level. NS is used to indicate nonsignificance. The indicated p value reflects the significance of the difference between the two trends. This convention is used in subsequent tables.

preexperimental period (0 to 5 days) and the first week score. The significance of difference between the experimental groups in their first week scores is also reported. While this difference may already be influenced by the experimental manipulation, it also reflects nonrandom, preexperimental differences between the aggressive TV and control groups. In the case of the general peer aggression measure, there is a fairly large initial difference which is not statistically significant. Nevertheless, this initial difference is a matter of concern, and a subsequent analysis will be reported in which the groups are equated on their first week scores.

The symbols in the last column pertain to the changes in the week-by-week median scores. The plus sign reflects a significant tendency for the scores to increase over the experimental period while the minus sign reflects a significant decline in the scores. In the case of the boys' homes, the difference between the two linear trends is statistically significant ($p < .04$). While it is of some interest that in the private school sample there is a significant decline in the control group, this decline is not significantly different from the change occurring in the aggressive TV group. It should also be noted that the final scores and overall median scores of the private school aggressive TV and control groups are quite comparable. (Unlike means, median scores cannot be averaged. Consequently, the overall median score does not reflect a simple average of the week-by-week medians. In addition, the overall median tends to be larger than the "average" of the individual medians. This occurs because the range is shifted upward; for example, there are more low aggression scores for a particular week than there are for the experimental period as a whole.)

In summary, Table 9 indicates that exposure to aggressive or nonaggressive television had no significant effect on the general peer aggression scores in the private school population but had a marked effect on the amount of aggression directed toward peers by children in the boys' homes. In the latter case, the aggressive TV group manifested much less aggressive behavior than the controls and also showed a reliable tendency to decline in aggression over the experimental period, which differed significantly from the trend in the control group. The significant decline in aggression toward peers in the boys exposed to aggressive content in television and the increase in aggression in the boys exposed to the control diet constitute the most important finding in this study. Much of the remainder of the analysis is concerned with determining the kinds of behavior and the kinds of youngsters for whom these experimental effects are strongest and those for whom the effects are weakest. There are also a number of technical and methodological refinements of analysis to strengthen the experimental implications of the data. Finally, since we did anticipate that many children would display some kind of increment in aggression in response to aggressive TV content, a number of analyses attempt to ascertain whether there is a subgroup which deviated from the overall finding.

The factor analysis of the behavior ratings indicated that aggression toward peers had both verbal and physical components. It was thus possible to determine whether the experimental effect was largely due to changes in verbal aggression, to changes in physical aggression, or to both. Both forms of peer aggression were greater in the control subjects. The differences in physical aggression toward peers tend to mirror those on the unfactored scale. The linear trend effect in the controls is stronger in the factored scale (Appendix Table B-1). In addition, the first week scores of the aggressive TV and control groups are closer than on the unfactored scale. In brief, the aggressive TV group displayed less physical aggression than the controls and showed a reliable decline relative to the controls. In the boys' homes, the aggressive TV and control groups began at a similar level of physical aggression but were widely divergent by the end of the sixth week. There was an interesting inversion during the third week which does not affect, however, the overall trends in the data. Particular caution is required in interpreting differences between the groups for any particular week since the behavior ratings show considerable fluctuation. At the same time, deviations from the major trends are of particular interest. We do not know whether this inversion was due to a random fight occurring among some of the aggressive TV boys or whether it was related in a subtle way to the influence of the aggressive TV programs. In contrast to the effects obtained for the boys' homes, the private school aggressive TV and control groups had almost identical scores on the physical aggression toward peers factor.

The differences between the aggressive TV and control groups in the amount of verbal aggression expressed toward peers are negligible in the private school scores and quite striking for the boys' homes sample (Appendix Table B-2). Unfortunately, there is also a significant difference between the aggressive TV and control groups in the very first week. Due to a significant decline in verbal aggression in the aggressive TV group, this difference is even larger for the last two weeks of the experiment. Another fact suggesting that the initial difference was not responsible for the experimental effect is that the first week's median for the controls is substantially greater than the median for the subsequent four weeks. Nevertheless, a more direct control of the possible effect of this initial difference is required and is presented later in this chapter.

Very little physical aggression was expressed toward authority figures by children in either the boys' homes or private schools (Appendix Table B-3). Nevertheless, consistent if slight differences do emerge. In the boys' home scores, the control group begins at the same level of aggression as the aggressive TV group but displays significantly more aggression over the experimental period. The aggressive TV group shows a tendency to decline on this measure but the trend is not significantly different from that in the control group. For the private school sample, the overall medians for the control and aggressive TV groups are the same. The aggressive TV group shows a significant increment in aggression, however; this trend differs at a borderline statistical level from the trend displayed by the controls. There is a significant initial difference which may have contributed to the difference in trends. This initial difference, which is in the same direction as that reported for the boys' homes on the verbal aggression toward peers measure, is associated with what appears to be a statistical regression effect rather than with an increase in the subsequent difference between the experimental groups.

The tendency for the controls in the boys' homes to increase in aggression and for the aggressive TV group to decline in aggres-

sion is very clearly reflected by scores on the verbal aggression toward authority measure (Appendix Table B-4). The aggressive TV
and control groups begin to diverge in the fifth week and steadily
grow further apart. It appears that the initial impact of differential
TV viewing is minor, but the effect becomes pronounced with sustained differential exposure.

A much lower incidence of aggressive behaviors occurred
in the private school sample than in the boys' home sample. In
addition, consistent with the other findings for the private school
subjects, the private school aggressive TV and control groups displayed similar patterns of aggressive verbal responses toward authority.

The finding that there were significant initial differences in the
boys' homes between the aggressive TV and control groups on the
verbal aggression toward peers factor requires further analysis.
While the first week score may already have been partly influenced
by the experimental treatment and while the weekly scores are
subject to considerable variation and can be misleading as to the
central tendency of the level of aggressive acting behavior, it is
clearly desirable to control statistically the possible effects of initial
differences. Our first approach to this problem was to divide the
population into three groups—high, middle, and low—on the basis
of their general peer aggression scores. (Because the scores were not
normally distributed (for example, there was a high frequency of 0
scores), the population was not divided into thirds but was sepa-
rated at natural breaks in the distribution, minimizing the variance
within each subdivision. Where the variable of initial level of behavior aggression is used in subsequent analyses of the pencil and
paper measure, it is this particular split that has been employed.)
The nonparametric analyses were then separately carried out for
the three groups for each of the behavior rating measures.

The initial medians and subsequent overall median general
peer aggression scores are presented in Table 10. The linear trends
are not enumerated in the table since the initial method matching
the groups ensured that the low groups would increase in aggression
and that the high groups would decline. Where a significant p value
is reported for the overall comparison, there was also a significant

Table 10. GENERAL AGGRESSION TOWARD PEERS

(with groups matched on initial level of peer aggression during preweek and first week)

Initial Level	Group	BOYS' HOMES			PRIVATE SCHOOLS		
		N	Overall Median	(1st Wk Median)	N	Overall Median	(1st Wk Median)
Low	Control	37	0.90	(0.0)	72	0.18	(0.0)
	Agg. TV	40	0.39	(0.0)	86	0.18	(0.0)
			p < .02			NS	
Middle	Control	26	1.44	(1.40)	55	0.81	(0.9)
	Agg. TV	38	0.92	(1.14)	49	0.71	(1.0)
			NS			NS	
High	Control	72	3.90	(5.25)	34	1.30	(3.22)
	Agg. TV	60	3.36	(5.05)	32	2.24	(2.91)
			p < .02			NS	

difference between the linear trends. The controls in the boys' homes exhibited more peer aggression than did the aggressive TV group at each initial level of aggression. The difference is highly significant for the low and high groups but does not attain statistical significance for the middle group. The lack of a statistically significant experimental effect in the middle group is in part due to the smaller sample size than in the low and high groups. In the private school high aggression group the aggressive TV group showed a substantially higher overall median than the controls. In this instance the median difference tends to exaggerate the actual difference between the two groups. (The means for the aggressive TV and control groups are 2.39 and 2.38.) Nevertheless, this trend is of interest since it is the first indication that exposure to aggressive content in television enhances aggressive behavior, although only in a small subsample of the experimental population.

The basic findings for the behavior rating factor scores are summarized in Table 11. These findings are similar to those of the general peer aggression scores prior to factor analysis, although they are less pronounced for some subgroups. For each subgroup there is at least one dimension or factor on which the boys' home control group is reliably more aggressive than the boys' home aggressive TV group. The differences are most pronounced in the low and middle groups; for the high sample a significant experimental effect was found only in verbal aggression toward peers.

It will be recalled that the control group obtained significantly higher verbal aggression toward peer scores than the aggressive TV group during the preweek and first week of the experimental period. This difference occasioned the present analysis in which the experimental groups are matched for initial level of peer aggression. A comparison of the initial median of each subgroup revealed that this matching procedure was successful in all instances except one—on the verbal aggression toward peer dimension the controls of the middle group were still initially higher than the aggressive TV group (p < .10). In order to eliminate this difference, the middle group was further subdivided into three groups. The mean for the control group is greater than the mean for the aggression TV group for each subdivision. Furthermore, an analysis of variance

Table 11. PHYSICAL AND VERBAL AGGRESSION TOWARD
PEERS AND AUTHORITY

(with groups matched on initial level of peer aggression during preweek and first week)

BOYS' HOMES

Factor	Initial Level	Con.	Agg. TV	p (diff.)
Physical Aggression Toward Peers	Low	.51	.25	NS
	Middle	.80	.74	NS
	High	2.45	2.30	NS
Verbal Aggression Toward Peers	Low	.77	.25	.01
	Middle	1.22	.50	.01
	High	3.21	2.51	.01
Physical Aggression Toward Authority	Low	.08	.01	.002
	Middle	.13	.05	.03
	High	.16	.24	NS
Verbal Aggression Toward Authority	Low	.89	.38	.002
	Middle	1.31	.51	NS
	High	1.65	1.65	NS

PRIVATE SCHOOLS

Factor	Initial Level	Con.	Agg. TV	p (diff.)
Physical Aggression Toward Peers	Low	.07	.03	NS
	Middle	.35	.39	NS
	High	.89	1.23	NS
Verbal Aggression Toward Peers	Low	.20	.14	NS
	Middle	.78	.59	NS
	High	1.16	2.00	NS
Physical Aggression Toward Authority	Low	.01	.02	NS
	Middle	.04	.02	NS
	High	.16	.14	NS
Verbal Aggression Toward Authority	Low	.23	.13	NS
	Middle	.39	.40	NS
	High	1.08	1.01	NS

shows the difference between these means to be highly significant. (A parametric procedure was possible here because the data met the assumptions for the analysis of variance.) From this analysis and the data presented in Table 11 we can reasonably exclude the possibility that initial differences between the aggressive TV and control groups were responsible for the significant experimental effects obtained in the boys' home sample. Even when the experimental groups are matched for initial peer aggression scores and divided into subsamples, significant differences are obtained on the behavior rating measures.

Turning to the private school results in Table 11, we find that none of the twelve comparisons are significant. However, the reversed trends in the high group on the physical and verbal aggression toward peer factors are intriguing. On the possibility that a more exact matching of the groups might highlight these differences, additional analyses were carried out for each behavior rating factor in which the aggressive TV and control groups were matched for their initial scores; for example, where the comparison was on the physical aggression toward peers scores, the matching was based on the initial scores on the physical aggression toward peers factor. The results remained very much the same, the greatest enhancement of differences occurring on the physical aggression toward peer factor with the highs attaining the .10 level. At the same time, the differences obtained for the boys' home experimental groups on this factor were considerably sharpened, two of the three differences becoming statistically significant with the probability for the third barely reaching the .05 level.

There were a number of variables in the population which might have influenced the experimental outcome. We analyzed some of these variables in order to identify subpopulations for whom the experimental effect was strongest and for whom it was weakest or absent and to clarify the psychological processes responsible for the experimental outcomes. One obvious variable is age. Three age groups participated in the experiment—high school students, junior high students, and a few high elementary students. The experimental results did not thus far indicate whether the difference in aggressive behavior produced by the experimental television diet holds for one or all the age groups or whether it is particularly strong among older or younger boys or whether it may even be reversed in some age group. The results of the analysis of the general peer aggression scores for the three age groups appear in Table 12. In the private school sample there is little difference between the control and aggressive TV group medians. In the boys' home sample the control median is substantially larger than the aggressive TV median at each level. Although the number of children in the primary grade groups was quite small, the overall difference between the control and aggressive TV groups is significant at the .10 level while the difference in linear trends over the experimental period is significant at the .02 level. Both the corresponding differences at the senior high level are statistically reliable; at the junior high level they are not reliable and, furthermore, are obscured by initial differences on this measure.

Analysis by age of the components of the peer aggression measure produced findings very similar to those in the overall index. The verbal aggression toward authority results were also similar. However, on analysis by age of the boys' home sample on the physical aggression toward authority measure, only the senior high group shows evidence of significant experimental effect. The differences at the primary level are large but not significant, possibly because of the small number of primary grade children in the study. The results for the private schools again show an absence of significant differences with the important exception that at the junior high school level the aggressive TV boys manifest a reliable increase in aggression which is significantly different from the change in the control group. It is possible that this is an artificial effect resulting from an initial difference (which, however, is not reliable) and the phenomenon of statistical regression to the mean. That the overall medians for the aggressive TV and control groups are identical suggests that this may well be the case. Nevertheless, this suggestion of a possible reversal in a private school subgroup of the striking general experimental finding in the boys' homes merits particular notice. If these suggestive trends in the analysis of the behavior rating differences in the private schools are buttressed by the findings for the questionnaire and other dependent measures, the hypothesis that aggression

Table 12. GENERAL AGGRESSION TOWARD PEERS
AS A FUNCTION OF GRADE LEVEL

BOYS' HOMES

	N	Overall Median	Linear Trend	1st Wk Median
Primary				
Control	(9)	15.06	+	4.00
Agg. TV	(13)	3.33	NS	5.00
p of diff.		< .10	< .02	NS
Jr. High				
Control	(46)	2.90	NS	2.00
Agg. TV	(36)	1.42	NS	0.40
p of diff.		< .10	NS	< .10
Sr. High				
Control	(60)	2.72	NS	2.13
Agg. TV	(73)	1.43	—	1.60
p of diff.		< .02	< .04	NS

PRIVATE SCHOOLS

	N	Overall Median	Linear Trend	1st Wk Median
Primary				
Control	(11)	0.85	—	1.98
Agg. TV	(9)	1.14	—	1.97
p of diff.		NS	NS	NS
Jr. High				
Control	(75)	0.63	NS	0.55
Agg. TV	(72)	0.87	NS	0.75
p of diff.		NS	NS	NS
Sr. High				
Control	(73)	0.35	NS	0.08
Agg. TV	(85)	0.30	NS	0.13
p of diff.		NS	NS	NS

is stimulated in certain children by exposure to an aggressive TV diet would acquire enhanced support.

The hypotheses guiding this study placed great emphasis on the role of personality factors in determining the impact of vicarious aggressive experience. It was assumed that exposure to aggressive content in television would have diverse effects, stimulating some children to further aggression, providing a substitute outlet for others, and leaving others unaffected. More specifically, our initial working hypothesis was that children low in initial aggressive tendencies were more likely to show an increase in aggressive behavior. There were restrictions on this hypothesis based on the relationship between overt and covert aggression. More complex analyses concerned with these restrictions and the joint effects of two measures of aggressive disposition are considered later.

The principal personality measures employed in the study were for aggression anxiety, covert hostility, overt hostility, neurotic undercontrol, and fantasy aggression. (Measures of conflict over aggression proved to be highly related to the first three instruments and will not be separately reported.) In addition, the sociometric or peer nomination of aggression measure was useful in designating individual differences in overt aggressive tendencies and, although it was not administered to the New York samples, it was included in the data analysis.

The distributions for each of these personality measures, administered prior to the experiment, were divided at the median and subjects were assigned to high or low groups for each measure. Separate analyses were then made of the experimental effects on high scorers and on low scorers. A summary of experimental differences in aggression toward peers for high and for low scores on the pertinent personality dimensions is presented in Table 13. To simplify the presentation of these data, only the overall median differences are presented. Each row of the table is based on a separate nonparametric linear trend and central tendency analysis. The figures in parentheses represent the number of boys in the immediately preceding and adjacent experimental groups. Since the median splits were based on the total sample, the boys' homes and private schools being grouped together, the numbers in the high-low splits for a particular experimental group (for example, boys' homes, control) may differ markedly.

Table 13 shows that the control and aggressive TV medians in the private schools are fairly similar and that none of the differences are significant. In the case of the boys' homes the differences are much larger and, equally important, they are consistent. At each personality level the control group displays more aggression toward peers than the aggressive TV group. However, the size of the difference between the medians and the level of statistical significance is systematically related to variations in personality dispositions. Within the boys' home sample the experimental effect is stronger in boys who are low in aggression anxiety, high in neurotic undercontrol, high in overt and covert hostility, and high in peer aggression nominations. That is, exposure to aggressive or non-aggressive TV has greatest impact on youngsters who have heightened aggressive tendencies coupled with weak inhibitory and ego controls. The one deviation from this pattern is the fantasy aggression split; low rather than high fantasy is associated with a larger experimental effect. In view of other considerations concerning the meaning of the fantasy measure, this apparent deviation can be interpreted in a manner consistent with the overall pattern. We suggest that the contrast of the relationship of the fantasy aggression measure to the experimental outcome with those of the other aggression measures provides a valuable insight into the psychological processes mediating the influence of television on behavior. We reserve full discussion of these findings for a subsequent chapter.

As an incidental note, it is of interest that in the boys' homes, where the range of peer aggression is much greater than in the private schools, high aggressive tendencies and weak inhibitory controls are associated with high peer aggression scores. This relationship is especially strong for the peer aggression nomination measure and, in this instance, applies to the private school sample as well. Regardless of experimental group, boys who score high on the peer aggression nomination measure display about twice as much aggressive behavior toward peers as boys who score low on the peer nomination measure. It will be recalled that the peer nomination measure is a sociometric procedure in which boys nominate other boys who fit a

Table 13. GENERAL AGGRESSION TOWARD PEERS
AS A FUNCTION OF EXPERIMENTAL TREATMENT AND
INITIAL PERSONALITY DIFFERENCES

BOYS' HOMES

Personality Traits	Control Overall Median	N	Agg. TV Overall Median	N	p of diff.
High Agg. Anx.	2.90	(81)	1.37	(81)	.02
Low Agg. Anx.	3.44	(52)	1.90	(54)	.004
High Neur. Undercon.	3.71	(64)	1.53	(65)	.002
Low Neur. Undercon.	2.66	(69)	1.68	(70)	NS
High Overt Host.	3.75	(54)	1.58	(60)	.002
Low Overt Host.	2.74	(79)	1.65	(75)	.04
High Covert Host.	3.54	(66)	1.71	(55)	.004
Low Covert Host.	2.71	(67)	1.50	(80)	.06
High Fant. Agg.	3.30	(56)	2.51	(54)	.10
Low Fant. Agg.	2.71	(69)	1.41	(75)	.01
High Peer Agg. Nom.	4.77	(35)	2.52	(40)	.001
Low Peer Agg. Nom.	2.16	(32)	.78	(10)	.08

PRIVATE SCHOOLS

Personality Traits	Control Overall Median	N	Agg. TV Overall Median	N	p of diff.
High Agg. Anx.	.53	(68)	.77	(64)	NS
Low Agg. Anx.	.53	(83)	.44	(87)	NS
High Neur. Undercon.	.67	(65)	.50	(74)	NS
Low Neur. Undercon.	.43	(86)	.51	(77)	NS
High Overt Host.	.48	(83)	.48	(72)	NS
Low Overt Host.	.57	(68)	.61	(79)	NS
High Covert Host.	.61	(67)	.50	(71)	NS
Low Covert Host.	.44	(84)	.51	(80)	NS
High Fant. Agg.	.50	(53)	.72	(58)	NS
Low Fant. Agg.	.70	(66)	.58	(51)	NS
High Peer Agg. Nom.	.84	(61)	.78	(77)	NS
Low Peer Agg. Nom.	.40	(92)	.31	(80)	NS

particular aggressive category. The peer nomination score is based on the number of times a particular boy was cited by other boys as displaying some aggressive behavior. The aggressive behavior toward peer score is based on the number and type of aggressive acts which the boy displayed during the course of the experiment. The validity of each measure is enhanced by the fact that there is substantial agreement between the measures, although they are based on very different procedures.

Analysis of the components of the peer aggression measure produces findings basically similar to Table 13, although the size and reliability of the experimental effect varies considerably. For the private school sample, the personality splits appear to have no bearing on the experimental outcome. None of the twenty-four comparisons of physical and verbal peer aggression made between the control and aggressive TV groups attain even the .10 level of statistical significance. The findings for the boys' homes again reflect the predominant trend of less aggressive behavior in the group exposed to aggressive television content than in the group exposed to the nonaggressive diet. On the physical aggression toward peers factor the differences are smaller and achieve satisfactory statistical reliability for only three groups—those high in neurotic undercontrol, those high in overt hostility, and those high in peer aggression nominations. The differences between the control and aggressive TV groups in verbal aggression toward peers are substantial and highly reliable. In every case the differences are significant for both highs and lows on the personality dimensions. Again the effects are stronger for the more aggressive and less inhibited boys but it nevertheless appears that personality factors play a less important role in determining the influence of the experimental treatment on verbal aggression than in determining the effect on physical aggression.

Aggression directed toward authority is a form of deviant behavior which is apt to be met with immediate and relatively severe punishment. Those who occupy authority roles in the social structure are not likely to be very tolerant of defiance of social norms particularly when defiance is expressed aggressively toward the authority figures themselves. One expects the frequency of aggressive acts toward authority, especially physically aggressive acts, to be much less than the frequency of similar acts directed toward peers. It is not rare for a subculture or a family to discourage aggression toward adults while reinforcing aggression toward peers (Feshbach, 1970). In view of the strong cultural restraints against the expression of aggression toward authority, it would not be very surprising if a relatively restricted situational factor such as change in television exposure had only a minimal effect on direct expressions of aggression toward authority figures. Nevertheless, in the boys' homes the experimental diet produced differences in aggressive responses to authority, and these differences were more pronounced for certain groups of children (see Appendix Tables B-5 and B-6). Youngsters who scored above the median in impulsiveness (neurotic undercontrol) were markedly influenced by the experimental TV diet; the aggressive TV group displayed significantly less physical aggression toward authority than did the controls. Boys above the median on the aggression scales (excepting the fantasy measure) displayed a comparable response. The findings for the analysis of verbal aggression toward authority are very much the same.

The importance of personality variables is very strongly reflected in these data. The unaggressive, inhibited, and controlled child shows little change in his response to authority as a function of TV diet. The diametrically opposite relationship of initial differences in fantasy aggression to the experimental outcome is most clearly reflected in these data: The child who is below the median in fantasy aggression is most reliably and strongly affected by exposure to the aggressive or the control TV diet. The personality analyses reported later, in which the relationship of fantasy aggression to the other measures and to the experimental effects is explored in greater depth, will be especially germane to the formulation of a theoretical account of the primary experimental data.

FIVE

Changes in
Attitudes, Values,
and Fantasies

$\mathbb{T}$he analysis thus far has concerned overt aggressive acts. In terms of social relevance, the measures of aggressive action are the critical experimental variables. From a psychological point of view, in terms of insights concerning the processes mediating aggressive behavior, the measures of aggressive attitude and value and of aggressive fantasy are no less important than the observations of direct aggressive activity. In assessing attitudes and values, a variety of procedures were employed to tap different aspects of the samples of feelings and cognitions involved in the evaluations of the various manifestations of aggression. These procedures, which were administered to all subjects before and after the experimental period, included a measure of aggressive values, a measure of preferences for particular hobbies, sports, and related activities which appear to have an aggressive component, a multiple-choice inventory which elicits evaluations of the morality and appropriateness of different responses to provoking situations, and a case history questionnaire which elicits opinions about the severity of punitive reactions meted out to a delinquent adolescent.

A sociometric procedure in which the participants enumerated peers whom they perceived as displaying particular aggressive dispositions and behaviors is less closely linked to the assessment of values and is best viewed as a more indirect indicator of aggressive activity than the behavior ratings. The measure of aggressive fantasy falls into neither the value nor the action area and occupies a category of its own. The instrument which assessed changes in attitudes toward a sample of aggressive and nonaggressive television programs was useful as an indicator of specific responses to the program diet rather than as a generalized value indicator. As has been previously noted, changes on the personality measures of overt and covert hostility, neurotic undercontrol, and aggression anxiety were not analyzed. While investigation of changes on these measures might be of some interest, the analysis was not made for several reasons, the most important being that there was no expectation of change on these broad personality dispositions. To the extent that these personality dispositions included value and attitudinal components on which changes were expected to occur, the change scores would overlap with the changes on our value measures, yielding little new information. However, as in the case of analysis of aggression toward peers and toward authority, attention was given to the possible influence of these personality factors on the effects of the experimental TV diet on aggressive attitudes and values.

A similar format was followed in analyzing each of the pre-post measures. First, possible differences between the aggressive TV group and the control group on the pretest, before the experiment was initiated, were checked. Change scores between the pre- and

posttests were then determined, and a comparison was made between the mean change in the controls and the mean change in the
aggressive TV group. Similar comparisons were carried out for each
of the major personality subgroups. Finally, the boys were divided
into private school and boys' home samples and into personality
subgroups, comparable but not identical to those used previously.
This last analysis made possible an assessment of the role of particular
personality factors in influencing the response of boys' home and
private school residents to the experimental treatment.

Perhaps the most salient aspect of these data is that the differences are not as impressive as those obtained in the analysis of
aggression toward peers and toward authority. Where significant
experimental effects were found they usually held for personality
subgroups rather than for the whole sample. However, except on
the measure of change in aggressive fantasy, the differences were
consistent with the behavior aggression data, the control subjects
tending to develop more favorable attitudes and values toward aggression than the boys exposed to aggressive content on television.
However, this statement must be carefully qualified. The results
differ for each measure; some experimental effects hold only for the
private schools or for the boys' homes or only for particular personality dispositions.

More specifically, the principal findings may be summarized:
(1) In both boys' homes and private schools, among boys high in
overt hostility and boys high on the peer nomination measure, control subjects manifested significantly greater increases on the aggressive values measure than did the aggressive TV group. (2) In both
boys' home and private school samples the controls manifested significantly greater increases in aggressive options on the situation test
than did the aggressive TV group. These data suggest that there
were at least some boys in the private schools who displayed a response to the experimental treatment similar to that of the boys'
home residents. Again, the experimental effect measure is strongest
for subjects high in peer nominations of aggression. Also, the increment is significantly greater in the control group for boys high in
aggression anxiety and for boys low in fantasy aggression. (3) No
significant differences between the aggressive TV and control groups

were found on the aggressive activity preference measure. (4) Differences in changes in severity of sentence advocated for a delinquent were small but in a direction consistent with the other experimental findings. When personality variables are taken into account, the control mean increment tends to be greater than the aggressive TV mean increment for boys high in neurotic undercontrol, low in overt hostility but high in covert hostility, and low in fantasy aggression. The association of low rather than high overt hostile tendencies with an experimental difference on this measure may be explained by the fact that punishing criminals is a socially sanctioned activity which the relatively nonaggressive boy may feel free to advocate.

In addition, (5) significant differences between aggressive TV and control groups on the peer nomination of aggression measure were obtained only for some personality groups. Reliably greater increments in peer nominations for aggression were manifested by the controls than by the aggressive TV group in the low aggression anxiety, high fantasy aggression subsample in the boys' homes. A similar effect was obtained for low overt hostility boys in the combined boys' home–private school population. These personality influences, particularly the dependence of the experimental effect on high rather than low fantasy aggression, are difficult to explain. (6) In contrast to the changes obtained on the other dependent measures, the controls manifested a significantly greater decrement in fantasy aggression than did the aggressive TV group. Exposure to the aggressive diet tended to maintain aggressive fantasies while those boys who did not watch aggressive television decreased their level of aggressive fantasy. Lacking external aggressive fantasy stimulation, they produced stories with less aggressive content than the boys who watched aggressive TV shows. This decrement in aggressive fantasy occurs in the controls, the group which increased in overt aggression. Possibly the removal of external fantasy stimuli (aggressive TV) coupled with a decline in internal aggressive fantasy is causally linked to the acting out of aggression. Differences between the control and aggressive TV groups in changes in aggressive fantasy were most profound in boys initially high in overt hostility, high in covert hostility, and high in physical aggression in fantasy. (7) Responses to the viewing habits measure, on which the participants expressed their degree of liking for a list of six TV shows with aggressive content and six shows with primarily nonaggressive content, indicated a greater preference for the aggressive programs although the nonaggressive programs were also liked. The boys' home controls showed an increase in liking of the nonaggressive shows following their experimental experience; this effect was greatest for boys considered highly aggressive by their peers. These findings strongly suggest that exposure to the nonaggressive television diet was not especially frustrating and they argue against the proposition that the controls increased in aggression because they were frustrated by their TV diet.

The nineteen items on the aggressive values index were averaged so that the mean score reflects the average extent of agreement with aggressive options, the range being from 1 to 4. A separate analysis was carried out for two subsets of items, one covering matters of personal aggression and the other covering aggressive alternatives in public policy. These two subsets yielded results similar to the total scale, and consequently, except where the subject findings differ markedly from the results for the total scale, only the findings for the latter are presented. These findings were analyzed in two stages. The initial approach compared the difference in change scores between the total aggressive TV and control samples and between the aggressive TV and control groups in each institution. The data indicate that while the overall mean for the controls is greater than that for the experimental group, the difference is small and not significant. In addition, neither individual institutional comparisons nor an analysis of variance separating the private schools from the boys' homes yielded a significant difference. However, the experimental effects become more evident when personality differences are taken into account.

The personality splits used for peer and authority aggression were also employed in analyzing the effects of the experimental treatment on aggressive values and other dependent measures. Table 14 compares the average aggressive values gain scores of the controls with those of the aggressive TV group. Two significant effects are reflected in this table. For subjects high in overt hostility, the control group mean is significantly greater than the aggressive TV group

Table 14. EFFECTS OF EXPERIMENTAL TREATMENT ON GAIN IN
AVERAGE AGGRESSIVE VALUE AS A FUNCTION OF
INITIAL SCORES ON PERSONALITY VARIABLES

	Overt Hostility	
	High	Low
Control	+ 0.19	+ 0.06
	(N = 74)	(N = 100)
Agg. TV	+ 0.03	+ 0.10
	(N = 64)	(N = 91)
	p < .05*	

	Covert Hostility	
	High	Low
Control	+ 0.10	+ 0.13
	(N = 93)	(N = 81)
Agg. TV	+ 0.06	+ 0.09
	(N = 90)	(N = 66)

	Aggression Anxiety	
	High	Low
Control	+ 0.13	+ 0.09
	(N = 100)	(N = 74)
Agg. TV	+ 0.08	+ 0.06
	(N = 81)	(N = 24)

	Neurotic Undercontrol	
	High	Low
Control	+ 0.08	+ 0.14
	(N = 85)	(N = 88)
Agg. TV	+ 0.03	+ 0.12
	(N = 80)	(N = 74)

	Physical Aggression in Fantasy	
	High	Low
Control	+ 0.12	+ 0.11
	(N = 101)	(N = 72)
Agg. TV	+ 0.09	+ 0.05
	(N = 91)	(N = 63)

	Peer Nomination	
	High	Low
Control	+ 0.21	+ 0.07
	(N = 45)	(N = 73)
Agg. TV	+ 0.04	+ 0.09
	(N = 53)	(N = 49)
	p < .03*	

*In this table and subsequent tables p values are indicated
only when the level of significance is .10 or less.

mean; the difference is insignificant for subjects low in overt hostility. A comparable effect is obtained for boys high and low in peer nomination of aggression. One cannot dismiss the possible influence of chance effects on nonindependent comparisons. It is important, however, that the two significant effects are consistent with the peer and authority aggression data. The findings indicate that boys who are initially aggressive tend to show a significant rise in aggressive values in response to a nonaggressive TV diet but not in response to an aggressive diet. Another factor contributing to the change on the aggressive values measure is grade level; the junior high school group is the only one which shows a significant difference. On all other change measures, findings for the different age groups are similar.

The personality splits reported in Table 14 are based on the mean of the personality scores; subjects falling above the mean were classified as high on that dimension and subjects falling below the mean were classified as low. The mean was used as the basis for the split primarily for convenience of computation although it did, in some instances, produce more homogeneous groupings than the median. In the later analysis of the data, in which analyses of variance were carried out, median splits were employed. In addition, several subjects were added to the later analyses after identification of some illegibly signed questionnaires. Thus, while the results of the initial and subsequent analyses are basically similar, they are not identical. Also, the second analysis permits one to determine whether the experimental difference obtained in a particular personality group occurs primarily in the boys' homes, in the private schools, or in both settings. However, the general tendency for the aggression scores on the questionnaire measures to increase on the posttest may obscure differences produced by the experimental treatment, including any interaction of the experimental treatment with the type of institution.

Reanalysis of the changes in aggressive values for different personality groups produced results very similar to the earlier findings. The controls showed a significantly greater increase in aggressive values than the aggressive TV group for boys high in overt hostility and for boys high in peer aggression nomination; the latter comparison attained only a .10 level of significance. This difference occurred in both the boys' home and private school samples. This suggestion of an increase in aggression in the private school controls relative to the private school aggressive TV group is interesting but demands more confirmation since it was not found in the analysis of the behavior ratings of the private school groups. While in general the changes in the components of the aggressive values scale mirrored the changes in the total scale, in one instance, that of boys high in neurotic undercontrol, a significant interaction between type of institution and experimental treatment appeared on the personal aggression component of the aggressive values scale. This interaction is noteworthy primarily because the aggressive TV group in the private schools showed more aggression than the controls. In the boys' homes, as on other measures, the controls manifested more aggression.

For the situation test of aggressive values the boys were presented with a series of possible reactions to a number of frustrating situations and were asked to indicate whether each would be a right or wrong reaction. Agreement with more aggressive alternatives was given greater weight and the item scores were then added together. There were several sizeable and significant differences between the control and aggressive TV groups on the pretest; this measure was subject to great fluctuation. The situation test scores for the total control and aggressive TV samples are almost identical on the pretest while on the posttest the mean of the control group is significantly larger than the mean of the aggressive TV group. This effect must be considered with some reservation since the change scores are not significantly different except for one institution. In Table 15 the effects of the experimental treatment are compared for different personality groups. Two differences are significant at the .05 level and one at the .10 level. The difference between the controls and the aggressive TV group for subjects low in aggression anxiety is greater than the difference for those high in aggression anxiety but the interaction is weak. Again the control mean is significantly greater than the aggressive TV group mean for subjects high in peer nomination of aggression while the means for the low peer nomination subjects differ slightly. The finding of a significant difference for the low fantasy aggression group provides additional

Table 15. EFFECTS OF EXPERIMENTAL TREATMENT ON
GAIN ON SITUATION TEST AS A FUNCTION OF
INITIAL SCORES ON PERSONALITY VARIABLES

Overt Hostility

	High	Low
Control	+ 5.02 (N = 73)	+ 4.13 (N = 77)
Agg. TV	+ 1.73 (N = 60)	+ 1.58 (N = 92)

Covert Hostility

	High	Low
Control	+ 3.91 (N = 83)	+ 5.37 (N = 67)
Agg. TV	+ 1.02 (N = 88)	+ 2.46 (N = 65)

Aggression Anxiety

	High	Low
Control	+ 3.40 (N = 80)	+ 5.90 (N = 70)
Agg. TV	+ 1.62 (N = 85)	+ 1.01 (N = 67) $p < .10$

Neurotic Undercontrol

	High	Low
Control	+ 3.67 (N = 82)	+ 5.64 (N = 68)
Agg. TV	+ 1.69 (N = 88)	+ 1.56 (N = 63)

Physical Aggression in Fantasy

	High	Low
Control	+ 3.74 (N = 88)	+ 5.93 (N = 61)
Agg. TV	+ 3.28 (N = 95)	− 0.95 (N = 56) $p < .02$

Peer Nomination

	High	Low
Control	+ 9.59 (N = 45)	+ 3.81 (N = 56)
Agg. TV	+ 1.77 (N = 59) $p < .03$	+ 3.62 (N = 44)

evidence of an increase in acceptance of aggressive options in the control but not in the aggressive TV group and is reminiscent of the significant differences in behavior ratings that occurred in this personality group.

The median split analysis of variance procedure produced very similar findings. The greater increase in aggressive options on the situation test of the controls than of the aggressive TV group is larger for the private schools than for the boys' homes. Moreover, separate comparisons between the controls and the aggressive TV subjects in the private schools yield statistically reliable differences. These data provide our best evidence that some boys in the private schools responded to the experimental treatment in a manner comparable to the typical response of the boys' home residents. This same difference appeared on the situation test when the entire boys' home and private school samples are analyzed without regard to personality differences. All groups showed an increment of aggression on retesting, especially the private school boys, but the increment in the controls is greater than the increment in the aggressive TV group.

The aggressive activity preference test was the most indirect measure of aggression employed. Although it was positively related to other indices of aggression, the correlations were low. However, it also proved to be the most stable measure, yielding the highest test-retest correlation. Activity preferences were apparently not greatly affected by the experimental treatment. The major significant differences are on the pretest. For the total sample, the pretest mean for the aggressive TV group is reliably higher than the control group mean, despite the random assignment of subjects to the aggressive TV and control treatments. (There is one other index, peer nomination of aggression, on which the initial scores of the aggressive TV group are reliably higher than those of the controls. On the other measures, including the various personality instruments, the initial means are similar.) It is also interesting that the mean for the comparison schools on this measure is significantly lower than that for the combined experimental sample (p < .05), since the comparison analysis was made to provide some index of the similarity of our experimental sample to a sample of boys attending school while living at home, who were presumed to be more typical of the general population. We shall point to significant differences on personality and attitude measures when these occur.

In the situation test the subjects were presented with a case history of a delinquent and were asked to recommend a length of jail sentence for him and to indicate their agreement with statements concerning recommended treatment. The sentence and treatment scores correlated substantially. Therefore we present the data only for the sentence score, which is readily interpretable. The means of the sentence score do not change very much from the pretest to the posttest. However, the personality splits presented in Table 16 indicate significant increases in severity of recommended sentence in the controls but not in the aggressive TV group. The difference in change scores between the control and aggressive TV groups is significant at the .05 level for boys high in neurotic undercontrol and those low in overt hostility; it is significant at the .10 level for boys high in aggression anxiety. The findings for the two aggression variables differ from the general pattern of interaction in that the experimental effect is most pronounced in boys with low or inhibited aggression rather than in boys high in aggression. The sentence recommended for the delinquent, perhaps more than any other measure, can be considered a socially sanctioned form of aggressive response, a category of behavior which Sears (1961) has labeled "prosocial aggression." The data suggesting that boys who are inhibited in overt aggressive behavior may tend to express increased aggressive tendencies in this socially approved manner are consistent with other findings relating to prosocial aggression.

The median split analyses of variance results neither support nor negate this interpretation. The control mean is greater than the aggressive TV mean for two personality subgroups—boys high in covert hostility and boys low in fantasy aggression. The experimental effects in the high covert hostility group hold only for the boys' homes. But boys' homes and private schools produce similar results when the changes in the low fantasy aggression group are analyzed; the difference is somewhat but not reliably stronger in the boys' homes.

Table 16. EFFECTS OF EXPERIMENTAL TREATMENT ON GAIN
IN RECOMMENDED SENTENCE AS A FUNCTION OF
INITIAL SCORES ON PERSONALITY VARIABLES

	Overt Hostility	
	High	Low
Control	+ 0.02	+ 0.28
	(N = 90)	(N = 113)
Agg. TV	+ 0.04	− 0.12
	(N = 77)	(N = 114)
		p < .05

	Covert Hostility	
	High	Low
Control	+ 0.19	+ 0.14
	(N = 111)	(N = 92)
Agg. TV	− 0.12	+ 0.05
	(N = 111)	(N = 81)

	Aggression Anxiety	
	High	Low
Control	+ 0.17	+ 0.17
	(N = 122)	(N = 80)
Agg. TV	− 0.20	+ 0.15
	(N = 112)	(N = 79)
	p < .10	

	Neurotic Undercontrol	
	High	Low
Control	+ 0.34	0.00
	(N = 106)	(N = 96)
Agg. TV	− 0.14	+ 0.06
	(N = 103)	(N = 87)
	p < .05	

	Physical Aggression in Fantasy	
	High	Low
Control	+ 0.05	+ 0.34
	(N = 122)	(N = 78)
Agg. TV	− 0.09	+ 0.01
	(N = 115)	(N = 75)

	Peer Nominations	
	High	Low
Control	− 0.15	+ 0.01
	(N = 58)	(N = 82)
Agg. TV	− 0.27	+ 0.31
	(N = 65)	(N = 53)

The peer nomination measure was administered to the California sample only. The mean for the aggressive TV group on the pretest is significantly greater than the control group mean, this difference being primarily evident at one boys' home and one private school. While the posttest means are almost identical, the difference in change scores fails to be statistically significant. The one significant difference in the change scores occurs in one of the boys' homes, where the controls manifested an increase and the aggressive TV group a decrease. The initial personality split comparisons failed to yield any significant effects on this measure. However, for several of the personality splits the experimental effect in the private schools is not the same as in the boys' homes; combining the two populations may obscure substantial differences between the control and aggressive TV groups. Since the overall analysis comparing boys' homes and private schools did not reveal any significant experimental effects, it appears that the relatively greater increment in peer aggression nomination in the control than in the aggressive TV group is dependent on the juxtaposition of a particular personality type and particular institutional setting.

For three personality subgroups—low aggression anxiety, high physical aggression in fantasy, and high overt hostility—the mean increase for the aggressive TV group is less than the increase for the controls in the boys' homes but is greater than the control mean increase in the private schools. However, the differences in the private schools are relatively small and are statistically insignificant while in the boys' homes the differences are reliable (.05 level) for the low aggression anxiety and high physical aggression in fantasy groups. For the low overt hostility group, the overall difference between the controls and aggressive TV subjects is significant. The mean increase in peer aggression nomination in both the private schools and boys' homes is smaller in the aggressive TV group than in the control group. The high physical aggression in fantasy results are an exception to the general finding of stronger experimental effect in low fantasy than in high fantasy groups. No explanation for this deviation from the general trend is immediately available. The personality data are clear, however, with regard to the principal experimental effect: Where there are significant differences in the boys' home sample, the aggressive TV group displays a smaller increment in aggressive behavior as judged by their peers than do the controls. In brief, the peer nomination measure, which is based on a very different procedure than the measures of aggressive values and the behavior ratings, yields data which are essentially consistent with the findings of the other measures.

The stories given in response to the Thematic Apperception Test cards administered at the beginning and completion of the experiment were scored for intensity of aggression and also for the number of physical aggression themes. These two scores are highly correlated. However, the measure of physical aggression in fantasy is less variable and yields more statistically significant differences. Although the intensity score yields a significant difference between the controls and aggressive TV group in the change scores for only one institution, the total mean physical aggression scores for the control and aggressive TV groups are significantly different at the .05 level, as are the means for two of the institutions. The controls show a significant decrement in fantasy aggression compared to a minimal change in the aggressive TV group. This is the only measure on which the control group decreases in aggression in comparison with the experimental subjects. The analyses of variance of the fantasy aggression change scores indicate that while the differences between the controls and aggressive TV groups is larger in the private schools —the private school controls show a large decrement—the experimental difference is not reliably greater in the private schools than in the boys' homes.

These data indicate that placing boys on a nonaggressive TV diet results in a decrease in physical aggression themes in fantasy while placing boys on an aggressive TV diet tends to maintain their aggressive fantasy level. To state these results in a form which suggests an interpretation, boys who have watched six weeks of TV shows in which relatively little physical aggression takes place are less likely to think of physical aggression in response to the stimulus cards than are boys who have watched six weeks of fighting and other forms of physical aggression. Table 17 indicates that this effect is most pronounced in boys who are high in overt hostility, covert hostility, and physical aggression in fantasy. These effects are less pronounced when the median split analyses of variance procedures

are used; in both boys' homes and private schools only the high
peer aggression nomination group shows a significant experimental
effect. There was one instance in which the pattern in the boys'
homes differed from that in the private schools. The largest change
in fantasy aggression in boys who were initially low in physical aggression fantasy occurred among the private school controls. They
differed reliably from the aggressive TV group and from the boys'
home controls.

While this latter finding does not lend itself to a ready theoretical interpretation, the findings for the other personality splits
suggest an interesting function for fantasy behavior. These results
in conjunction with the previous findings indicate that boys who
are initially aggressive respond to the control condition with an
increase in aggressive values and in acting out of aggression but with
a decrement in aggressive fantasy in comparison with their response
to the aggressive TV condition. The data suggest that aggressive
fantasy which is positively but not highly correlated with overt aggressive expression may partly control that expression.

A viewing habits measure consisting of a list of six TV shows
with aggressive content and six programs with primarily nonaggressive content was administered at the beginning and at the conclusion
of the experiment. The boys were asked to indicate on a four-point
scale the frequency with which they watched these shows and on a
five-point scale the extent to which they liked the shows. The frequency score did not prove fruitful. The posttest was confusing for
the boys; some boys responded with the frequency with which they
watched the show during the experimental period and others described the preexperimental period. The like-dislike index was not
subject to this difficulty. To the extent that the listed programs
are representative of the aggressive and nonaggressive programs,
changes in liking of these shows can be taken as crude approxima-
tions of the effects of the experimental treatment on preferences
for aggressive and nonaggressive TV shows. The mean ratings for
the aggressive programs show that the boys like these programs.

While the mean like-dislike ratings of the nonaggressive
shows reflect a positive attitude toward these shows, they are significantly lower than the means for the aggressive shows. At one institu-

Table 17. EFFECTS OF EXPERIMENTAL TREATMENT ON GAIN
IN PHYSICAL AGGRESSION IN FANTASY AS A FUNCTION OF
INITIAL SCORES ON PERSONALITY VARIABLES

Overt Hostility

	High	Low
Control	− 0.50	− 0.24
	(N = 86)	(N = 116)
Agg. TV	+ 0.07	− 0.15
	(N = 79)	(N = 118)
	p < .02	

Covert Hostility

	High	Low
Control	− 0.49	− 0.18
	(N = 111)	(N = 91)
Agg. TV	+ 0.12	− 0.31
	(N = 116)	(N = 82)
	p < .001	

Aggression Anxiety

	High	Low
Control	− 0.41	− 0.23
	(N = 123)	(N = 78)
Agg. TV	− 0.10	− 0.02
	(N = 114)	(N = 83)
	p < .10	

Neurotic Undercontrol

	High	Low
Control	− 0.38	− 0.30
	(N = 106)	(N = 95)
Agg. TV	0.00	− 0.14
	(N = 106)	(N = 90)
	p < .10	

Physical Aggression in Fantasy

	High	Low
Control	− 0.85	+ 0.38
	(N = 121)	(N = 82)
Agg. TV	− 0.42	+ 0.53
	(N = 123)	(N = 75)
	p < .02	

Peer Nomination

	High	Low
Control	− 0.19	− 0.40
	(N = 56)	(N = 81)
Agg. TV	+ 0.17	+ 0.03
	(N = 70)	(N = 53)
		p < .10

tion the mean is particularly high and is not significantly different from the mean of the aggressive shows; the boys at this institution simply like television. The control mean for the total sample tends to be greater than the aggressive TV group mean ($p < .10$) on the pretest and while the difference on the posttest is highly reliable, the difference of the change scores is not significant. The controls show a reliable gain in liking of nonaggressive shows in comparison with the change in the aggressive TV group in two of the four boys' homes in which the controls display significantly greater peer aggression than the aggressive TV group. The comparison of the boys' homes with the private schools reflects an overall increase in liking of nonaggressive shows in the boys' home controls which is reliably greater than the decrement in the private school controls.

In the initial analysis of the data, the relationship between personality factors and changes on this pre-post rating measure was not examined. However, in the subsequent analysis these relationships were investigated and several differences between the aggressive TV and control groups emerged. In all these comparisons the response of the boys' homes sample to the experimental treatment differs from that at the private schools. High overt hostility subjects in the boys' homes show little change in ratings of aggressive shows if they have been exposed to aggressive television and a small increment if they were in the control group; just the reverse relationship is displayed by the private school high overt hostility group. The child who is low in overt hostility responds in another fashion to the experimental treatment. His rating of aggressive shows increases if he is from the boys' homes and has been exposed to aggressive TV but declines if he is a private school child and has been exposed to aggressive content in TV. This interaction is highly complicated and is not easily interpreted. It appears that, if the private school child has an aggressive disposition, he will find aggressive shows to his liking on extensive exposure to them; if he is nonhostile, exposure will reduce his liking for such shows. The adolescents and preadolescents in the boys' homes typically watched more TV before the initiation of the experiment than did the private school subjects. Those boys who were high in initial hostility have already seen a good deal of aggressive TV, rate it highly initially, and show little change after repeated exposure. The boys low in hostility find the programs less compatible with their personal inclinations but they are less critical of TV than their private school counterparts and tend to like programs they see.

The one interaction between personality and experimental treatment in the ratings of the nonaggressive shows is suggestive. In the boys' homes, controls high in peer nomination of aggression show an increase in liking while similar subjects in the aggressive TV group show a decline. This personality subgroup in the boys' homes manifested consistent and reliable differential response in aggressive behavior and values to the experimental treatment. The fact that the controls display an increment in their liking of non-aggressive programs suggests a favorable response to the programs they observed and that the greater aggression they manifested is not attributable to dislike for the program diet. More direct evidence on this point is presented later.

SIX

Influence
of Fantasy

The previous chapters were concerned with effects; the present chapter is concerned wtih mediating processes. The methodology is very much the same; only the emphasis differs. Our analyses here are concerned with complex combinations of personality factors and with other variables. We hope to clearly establish the psychological significance of exposure to aggressive episodes on television. It will be recalled that the initial experimental hypotheses predicted various interactions between overt and covert aggressive tendencies. It was anticipated that the only children who would decrease in behavioral aggression as a result of exposure to the aggressive TV diet would be children who displayed both strong overt

113

and strong covert aggressive tendencies. It was further anticipated that children initially low in overt aggression would respond to exposure to aggressive content in television with an increment in aggressive behavior. The analyses already reported make it highly improbable that this interactional analysis can yield results which accord with the experimental hypotheses, especially with those predicting a stimulation effect. Nevertheless, it is still of interest to examine the possible effects of different combinations of overt and covert aggressive tendencies.

Of the predispositional measures administered, the overt hostility questionnaire and the peer nomination index are most appropriate for assessing overt aggressive tendencies. Since the peer nomination index was not given in two of the four boys' homes, the number of subjects in some of the personality constellations is quite small. Hence, the overt hostility scale is the primary measure considered. Initially we assumed that the TAT-type fantasy measure would provide a sensitive indicator of covert aggressive impulses or aggressive drive. This assumption has been basic to the clinical use of the Thematic Apperception Test and, in addition, has some foundation in experimental studies of changes in thematic fantasies following aggression arousal. We must now sharply modify this assumption. Nevertheless, the fantasy measure remains the most widely accepted measure of covert aggressive impulses and the best one available to us.

It was found that the experimental TV diets had little effect on the aggressive behavior of boys high in covert hostility (fantasy aggression) and low in overt hostility. The strongest effects were produced in boys low in fantasy aggression and high in overt hostility. The findings are based on the boys' home sample, which chiefly accounted for the experimental results. (There were no significant differences in the private school sample.) In the boys' homes the overtly hostile boy who has few aggressive fantasies is most prone to display the experimental effect. Boys in the homes who engage in more hostile fantasies but who are not overtly hostile do not show as great an experimental effect.

The findings are quite similar when the peer nomination for aggression measure is utilized as a measure of aggressive tendencies.

It should be noted, however, that private school boys initially high in fantasy aggression (covert hostility) and high in peer nominations for aggression showed more verbal aggression toward authority figures if they were in the aggressive TV group than if they were in the control group. Although this is a somewhat complex finding it merits discussion because it represents a rare case of apparently greater aggression in a subgroup exposed to aggressive TV programs. On examination, however, it turned out that significant differences could not be found for this subgroup on other behavior comparisons. In fact, opposite effects were obtained on some of the before-after change score measures. Therefore, this isolated finding may have been due to chance. A concluding analysis in the chapter of prior TV viewing behavior indicated that the experimental effects were as significant for boys who in the past did not watch much TV as for those who had watched a medium or considerable amount of television. It therefore appears unlikely that the experimental effect is due to the controls experiencing frustration as a result of having been removed from their prior TV diet.

As an initial step in the analysis of varying combinations of overt and covert aggression, the subjects were categorized as high or low in fantasy aggression and high or low in overt hostility, depending on whether their scores fell above or below the medians for each measure. Four personality subgroups were thereby generated: low fantasy aggression, low overt hostility; low fantasy aggression, high overt hostility; high fantasy aggression, high overt hostility; high fantasy aggression, low overt hostility. A separate nonparametric trend analysis of the behavior rating measures was carried out for each of these personality combinations. The results, while in accord with the findings of the single personality dimension comparisons, are intriguing. None of the twenty comparisons made within the private school population approaches statistical reliability and, in general, the control and aggressive TV medians for the private school boys are fairly close. As might be anticipated from previous data, the median aggression scores for the boys' home aggressive TV groups tend to be lower than the median aggression scores for the corresponding boys' home control groups. The reliability of these differences is less than in previous comparisons, largely because of the lower number of subjects in each personality sub-group. Furthermore, since the variations in numbers of subjects can influence the reliability of the obtained differences, one must be cautious in attributing theoretical significance to statistically stated levels of significance. Here, one must be guided by the size of the obtained difference as well as by its statistical reliability.

Despite these cautions, the data clearly indicate that the experimental variation in TV diet had least effect on those children in the boys' homes who were initially high in fantasy aggression and low in overt hostility. The data also suggest that the effects are strongest for boys low in fantasy aggression but high in overt hostility. Significant effects are found on some of the behavior aggression ratings for each of the other two subgroups, and in some instances the median differences are as large as or larger than the median for the low fantasy, high overt hostility subgroup. Consequently, we can only tentatively suggest that this particular combination of personality variables in a boys' home resident makes him especially responsive to differences in TV diet. (The single variable personality analysis indicated that children low in aggressive fantasy were more affected by the experimental manifestations than children high in aggressive fantasy and that children high in overt hostility were more influenced than children low in overt hostility. It may be that a ceiling effect is operative here, so that the combination of variables does not increase the effect of each single factor.)

Separate analyses for each of the fantasy aggression, overt hostility subgroups were also carried out for the before and after dependent measures. Inasmuch as there are fewer subjects available for the analysis of the change scores than for the behavior rating analysis, the reduction and variation in size of the personality subgroups reduces the likelihood of obtaining significant differences, especially in view of the variability of the change scores. Furthermore, the variation in size of the different subgroups could be a critical factor in determining differences in the reliability of experimental effects. Therefore, it is not surprising that the fantasy aggression, overt hostility breakdown yielded little new data or additional evidence that the low fantasy, high overt hostility personality combination plays a special role. For example, for changes in peer aggression nomination, the mean increment in the boys' homes low fantasy aggression, high overt hostility control group is .84 compared to .53 in the low fantasy aggression, high overt hostility aggressive TV group; the high fantasy aggression, high overt hostility comparison yields corresponding means of 1.1 and −.13, which are reliably different ($p < .05$). Yet on changes in recommended sentence for the delinquent, the largest differences occur in the low fantasy aggression, low overt hostility boys (boys' home control, $M = +.30$, boys' home aggressive TV, $M = −.45$; private school control, $M = +.53$, private school aggressive TV, $M = +.01$); the differences between the controls and aggressive TV groups for the combined boys' home and private school samples and for the boys' home sample alone are significant at the .05 level. For reasons already noted, these data are difficult to interpret.

The power of the statistical procedure could be enhanced by incorporating, in one overall analysis of variance, the two personality dimensions, the boys' homes-private school variable and the major experimental variable. Apart from the difficulties of interpreting higher order interactions and of programing, an analysis of this scope, with unequal N's, proved to be quite costly and difficult and, in view of the limited additional information that may have resulted, was not carried out.

Use of the peer aggression nomination measure as an index of initial overt aggressive tendencies exaggerates problems of interpretation because of the great reduction in sample size. Nevertheless, this analysis was made and is commented on here primarily because of one deviant finding. The results, in the main, paralleled those obtained for the fantasy aggression, overt hostility analyses. The strongest differences between the aggressive TV and control subjects in behavioral aggression scores occur in boys from the boys' homes who were initially low in physical aggression in fantasy and high in peer nomination of aggression. Again, in the boys' homes sample, the least significant effects are found in the high fantasy, low peer aggression nomination boys. Although none of the behavior rating comparisons for the change score comparisons of the fantasy aggression, overt hostility subgroups in the private school approached statistical reliability, one statistically significant difference was obtained on a behavior rating measure when the peer aggression nomination measure was substituted for the overt hostility scale. The difference occurred in high fantasy, high peer agg. nomination boys who displayed significantly more physical aggression toward peers when exposed to aggressive content in television than when exposed to nonaggressive content. The presence of one significant difference in the private school population out of twenty behavior rating comparisons may be a chance finding. It is indeed difficult to understand why none of the behavior rating factors reflected this experimental difference. At the same time, in view of the possible implications of the overall data, it is important to attend to any deviant result.

If similar experimental effects were obtained for this personality subgroup on the change score measures of aggression, we would be inclined to minimize the role of chance, even though the comparisons are not completely independent of each other. The change score data fail to show any differences reflecting reliably greater increments in the aggressive TV group than in the controls. In fact, on a number of measures, the private school high fantasy aggression, high peer nomination of aggression aggressive TV group displayed a decrement in aggression compared with their controls. On the situation test, the difference between the high fantasy aggression, high peer nomination control and aggressive TV groups for the combined private school and boys' home populations approached statistical significance ($p < .10$; private schools: controls +.54, aggressive TV −.35; boys' homes: controls +.26, aggressive TV −2.46). On the aggressive activity preference measure, this same difference for the combined high fantasy, high peer aggression nomination subsample was significant at the .05 level (private schools: controls +.54, aggressive TV −.31; boys' homes: controls +1.72, aggressive TV −2.5). There is a reversal in this subgroup on the recommended sentence measure (private schools: controls −.49, aggressive TV −.04; boys' homes: controls −.76, aggressive TV +.01). None of the individual comparisons for the private school subsample on these three measures are reliable, while the difference for the boys' homes subsample is significant for the aggressive activity preference measure ($p < .05$), approaches significance for the situation test ($p < .10$), and is insignificant for the recommended sentence measure. The most reasonable interpretation of these changes in the private school sample is that they are essentially caused by chance, and reflect neither a reliable increment nor a reliable decrement in the aggressive TV boys or in the controls.

The evidence that an aggressive TV diet, relative to a nonaggressive diet, results in a decrement in aggression in the boys' homes population, can be interpreted by several different theoretical approaches. We shall consider here one possibility and examine one analysis that bears upon it. In considering the effects of placing some children on an aggressive TV diet and others on a nonaggressive diet, one is inclined to look to the aggressive diet as the source of any experimental differences. Thus catharsis and modeling are both processes which are mediated by the aggressive diet, leading in the former case to a decrement and in the latter case to an increment in aggressive behavior. The implicit assumption in either case is that the experimental changes result from exposure to a heavy concentration of aggressive television content. However, one could consider the control diet the primary source of the experimental effect; that is the absence of aggressive content may be the critical factor. If witnessing aggression on TV has served in the past to partially express and modulate aggressive impulses, then removal of this support might release aggressive behavior tendencies.

One matter pertinent to this issue is the nature and extent of the television diet of the boys prior to the experiment. Unfortunately, prior television viewing habits were not adequately surveyed. A very gross estimate of frequency of prior TV viewing can be made from the responses to the viewing habits measure, in which subjects indicated their preference for selected TV programs and the frequency with which they viewed them. While the programs could be categorized into an aggressive and nonaggressive group, the correlations did not neatly fall into two arrays, and, in addition, it was felt that all the programs should be used in arriving at an estimate of TV viewing behavior. A total score, based on the frequency with which the twelve listed programs were viewed, was derived. Subjects were then categorized into high, medium, and low frequency groups depending on whether they fell into the approximate upper, middle, or lower third of the distribution.

When the before-after changes were separately analyzed for each frequency level, the number of significant differences was reduced. Again, the smaller effects for the change scores, the variability of these scores, and the sharp reduction in size of sample when the boys' homes and private school populations are each divided into three parts severely limit the possible fruitfulness of this analysis. In contrast, the analysis of the behavior rating scores as a function of initial frequency of watching TV provided some interesting findings. These are most evident in the peer aggression data although comparable trends are discernable on the authority aggression factors. The analysis of the general peer aggression ratings is presented in Table 18. In all three frequency levels in the boys' homes, the control median is greater than the aggressive TV median. Probably little should be made of the fact that the difference is not significant for the high frequency group (especially since the controls have reliably higher authority aggression scores than do the aggressive TV group). Also, as Table 18 indicates, the difference in verbal aggression for the highs is significant at the .10 level and the difference in the linear trend effect in physical aggression toward peers is significant at the .04 level. What is of theoretical importance, however, is the finding of a significant effect for the low frequency group. To the extent that the frequency with which the twelve programs were viewed can be taken as an index of overall TV viewing, these data would argue against a withdrawal explanation of the experimental findings. The low frequency subjects were not addicted to TV but were nevertheless influenced by the difference in TV diet. These data argue against a frustration explanation of the findings; if the controls were frustrated because they were taken off their favorite aggressive TV programs, then the experimental effect should be maximal in, and perhaps restricted to, the high frequency group. However, boys whose prior TV viewing frequencies appear to be less were just as affected by the experimental treatment.

The findings also indirectly bear on the theoretical propositions concerning the absence of aggressive TV fantasy content in

Table 18. EXPERIMENTAL DIFFERENCES IN AGGRESSIVE
BEHAVIOR AS A FUNCTION OF INITIAL FREQUENCY OF
WATCHING TV

GENERAL AGGRESSION TOWARD PEERS

BOYS' HOMES

	Group	N	Median	Linear Trend
High	Control	(39)	2.47	+
	Agg. TV	(28)	1.44	NS
	p of diff.		NS	NS
Middle	Control	(24)	3.50	NS
	Agg. TV	(38)	1.63	NS
	p of diff.		.01	NS
Low	Control	(47)	3.40	NS
	Agg. TV	(50)	1.86	—
	p of diff.		.04	NS

PRIVATE SCHOOLS

	Group	N	Median	Linear Trend
High	Control	(30)	.63	NS
	Agg. TV	(23)	.83	NS
	p of diff.		NS	NS
Middle	Control	(43)	.38	NS
	Agg. TV	(30)	.60	NS
	p of diff.		NS	NS
Low	Control	(46)	.84	—
	Agg. TV	(55)	.71	NS
	p of diff.		NS	NS

PHYSICAL AGGRESSION TOWARD PEERS

		BOYS' HOMES		PRIVATE SCHOOLS	
	Group	Median	Linear Trend	Median	Linear Trend
High	Control	1.27	+	.28	NS
	Agg. TV	1.08	—	.39	NS
	p of diff.	NS	.04	NS	NS

Table 18. (cont.)

		Median	Linear Trend		
	Control	1.72	NS	.14	NS
Middle	Agg. TV	1.20	NS	.23	NS
	p of diff.	.06	NS	NS	NS
	Control	1.69	+	.43	NS
Low	Agg. TV	1.30	—	.37	NS
	p of diff.	.10	.02	NS	NS

VERBAL AGGRESSION TOWARD PEERS

		BOYS' HOMES		PRIVATE SCHOOLS	
	Group	Median	Linear Trend	Median	Linear Trend
	Control	1.84	NS	.56	NS
High	Agg. TV	.92	NS	.61	NS
	p of diff.	.10	NS	NS	NS
	Control	3.01	NS	.44	NS
Middle	Agg. TV	.91	NS	.69	NS
	p of diff.	.002	NS	NS	NS
	Control	3.37	NS	.73	NS
Low	Agg. TV	1.69	—	.50	NS
	p of diff.	.02	NS	NS	NS

the controls and the added opportunity for vicarious aggressive expression possibly provided by the aggressive TV diet. The previous findings, particularly those bearing on the role of TAT fantasy, have pointed to the cognitive functions that aggression in television may serve in helping to regulate and delay aggressive behavior. The significant effects observed in the low frequency subjects suggest that a substitute, vicarious aggressive effect may also operate for some subjects.

SEVEN

Further
Considerations

Throughout the presentation of the data, reference has been made to methodological issues; several analyses were generated by essentially methodological questions. Nevertheless, there are a number of issues pertaining to the administration of the two television diets and the before-after dependent measures that have not yet been considered or which warrant further examination. The greater behavioral aggressiveness of the boys exposed to the non-aggressive diet than of the boys who watched primarily aggressive content is a striking experimental finding. However, no experiment is without possible sources of bias or constant error and it is es-

123

sential to review what data is available that bears on methodological considerations. The analyses reported here are basically concerned with the extent of participation in the experiment, conformity with and reaction to the program diets, and relationships among the measures of aggression.

A number of boys failed to complete the experiment; it is pertinent to examine the possible effects that differential participation in the study may have exerted on the experimental outcomes. (It should be noted that most of the boys who failed to complete the experiment or to take the pretest came from two of the private schools.) A related factor could be differential reporting of observations for the control and aggressive TV groups. The mean numbers of behavior ratings submitted for the aggressive TV group and for the control group are roughly equal. Even when further subdivided on the basis of boys' homes and private schools, the mean numbers of behavior ratings for the two experimental conditions are very similar. It seems, then, that treatment differences were not due to difference in the reporting of behavioral data. The data further indicate that the differences obtained in aggressive behavior as a function of the experimental treatment were not biased by differential participation in the experiment. This finding is consistent for both boys' homes and private schools. Considering, in addition, the nonbehavioral measures of attitude, value, and personality predisposition, it is generally true that the experimental effects cannot be attributed to differential rates of participation between the aggressive TV and control subjects.

It should be noted that the boys in each group did watch the types of shows they were assigned to watch. There was only a minimal amount of watching shows other than those assigned. In general the boys liked the programs they watched. Seventy per cent of the control programs were rated as "liked very much or fairly" and only 15 per cent as "disliked." Seventy-seven per cent of the aggressive programs were rated "liked very much or fairly" and only 8 per cent as "disliked." Thus, while the aggressive shows may have been liked a little better, most of the shows in both experimental conditions were liked. The aggressive shows, as might be expected, aroused more reported excitement, fear, nervousness, upset, anger, and sadness than the control shows. The control programs elicited more reported good and happy feelings. Again this argues that the control subjects enjoyed the shows they watched and found most of them interesting. The amounts of television viewing by the two groups were very close to equal.

Test-retest correlations proved to be somewhat lower than expected, seldom exceeding .50. However, the reliabilities are high enough for the measures to reflect the effects of the experimental variable. Correlations among the tests show that overt hostility, covert hostility, and neurotic undercontrol are related to each other and, with some exceptions, show similar relationships to other variables. The aggressive activity preference measure, aggressive values measure, peer nomination measure, and situation test are related to each other and also relate positively to overt hostility, covert hostility, and neurotic undercontrol. Some evidence for the validity of the peer nomination of aggression measure is provided by its correlation with the fantasy and questionnaire measures of aggression.

Two comparison schools, whose student bodies lived at home, were used to establish the degree of similarity of the experimental population to typical school populations. In general, the means for the comparison schools are similar to those of the experimental population on all the personality measures except the conflict index. Also, control and aggressive TV groups were, on the whole, initially similar on premeasures except at Pacific Lodge Home, which had a larger number of aggressive boys in the aggressive TV treatment. The greater behavior aggression ratings earned by the control subjects are all the more striking since the aggressive TV subjects in at least one of the boys' schools may have started out being more aggressive. In summary, it does not seem that the factors considered in this chapter biased the experimental outcome.

Turning to each of these issues in greater detail, one matter of concern is that many boys failed to complete the experiment. If for some reason there was a difference between the subjects who left the aggressive TV group and those who left the control group, so that the former tended to be more aggressive boys, the difference could influence the experimental findings. Of all the dependent measures, the behavior rating findings are least likely to be affected by subjects departing at different times from the experiment. This is because the average peer aggression and authority aggression scores were derived by dividing the sum of the aggression ratings by the number of behavior rating forms submitted for that child. Furthermore, most of the boys who failed to complete the experiment or who did not take the pretest and entered the experiment after it had begun came from the Army and Navy Military Academy and the Cate School, two of the three private schools which did not conform to the overall experimental finding. Consequently, differences in the length of participation in the project are primarily germane to these institutions and are only minimally related to the four boys' homes settings in which significant experimental effects were obtained.

One possible reflection of differential participation is the mean number of behavior ratings and program reaction forms for the control and aggressive TV groups. These are separately presented in Table 19. Subjects who took the pretest but not the posttest had fewer behavior ratings and fewer program ratings than those who took both tests. Subjects who took only the posttest had approximately the same number of behavior ratings as those who took both tests but submitted fewer program ratings. Subjects who missed the pretest also missed a fair number of TV programs or else they simply did not always bother to submit program reaction forms. With regard to the behavior ratings, what is most germane is that the mean numbers of behavior ratings submitted for the controls and for the aggressive TV group are comparable. When these data are broken down by boys' homes and private schools, the control and aggressive TV group means within each population remain very close. Comparisons between the boys' homes and the private schools show a greater mean number of behavior ratings for the private school groups. This difference is in large part because fewer pre- and postexperimental behavior ratings were made in the New York institutions.

There was little difference in the mean number of program reaction forms submitted by the boys' homes and private school groups and considerable variation within each group. It should be noted that the mean number of program reaction forms only par-

Table 19. Mean Number of Behavior Ratings and Program Reaction Forms

		Pretest Only	Posttest Only	Both Tests
Number of Behavior Ratings	Control Mean	24.33	30.52	30.93
	N	(54)	(52)	(203)
	Agg. TV Mean	22.22	31.12	30.36
	N	(54)	(51)	(192)
Number of Nonaggressive Program Reaction Forms	Control Mean	17.50	17.31	32.12
	Agg. TV Mean	1.94	1.47	3.44
		$p < .001$	$p < .001$	$p < .001$
Number of Aggressive Program Reaction Forms	Control Mean	0.83	0.60	0.87
	Agg. TV Mean	15.14	13.47	21.94
		$p < .001$	$p < .001$	$p < .001$

tially reflects the amount of television watched by the boys in connection with the experiment. First, these means are based on a 90 per cent sampling of the TV program reaction forms submitted. Second, signatures on a number of forms were illegible and the forms could not be assigned to the proper individuals. Finally, the boys did not religiously complete a form for each program they watched. In the two New York institutions they were only required to complete one program reaction form a day; in the California institutions they were encouraged but not compelled to submit a program reaction form after each program viewing. In general, we attempted to minimize any frustration ensuing from the implementation of the experiment. Program reaction forms were always available and the boys were asked to complete them but no sanctions were imposed if they failed to do so. Toward the same end, while the boys were required to watch a minimum of six hours of TV a week, there was no maximum limit, provided they watched programs from the TV diet to which they were assigned. It appears from Table 19 that the boys in the control group viewed much more television than did the boys in the aggressive TV group. This difference is deceptive because each program rating reflects a particular program rather than amount of time, and a much higher proportion of nonaggressive programs than aggressive programs are half-hour in length. What is most apparent is the very sharp difference in the type of program witnessed by the aggressive TV and control samples, this difference reflecting the experimental manipulation of program diet. Some cross-over was permitted. In addition, some leakage was inevitable and boys assigned to the control diet watched a few aggressive TV programs, and the aggressive TV group watched a few nonaggressive programs. In the case of one particular aggressive program, "Batman," permission was granted to the control group boys at Institutions B and C to watch the program since many of them had requested it and we wished to avoid creating any resentment or irritation because of the experimental assignment. In any case, the amount of leakage or cross-over was minimal.

Table 20 presents peer and authority aggression means as functions of the experimental treatment and participation in the pre-

Table 20. Average Aggression Toward Peers and
Authority as Functions of Experimental Treatment and
Participation in the Pretest and Posttest

			Peer Aggression	Authority Aggression
Subjects With Pretest Only	Control	Mean	2.39	1.05
		N	(54)	(54)
	Agg. TV	Mean	1.19	1.08
		N	(54)	(54)
			$p = .10$	$p > .10$
Subjects With Posttest Only	Control	Mean	1.54	.96
		N	(52)	(52)
	Agg. TV	Mean	.66	.64
		N	(51)	(51)
			$p < .05$	$p > .10$
Subjects With Pre- and Posttests	Control	Mean	3.36	1.51
		N	(203)	(195)
	Agg. TV	Mean	2.06	1.10
		N	(192)	(192)
			$p < .01$	$p < .02$

test and posttest. The mean aggression scores for subjects who took
only one test are considerably less than the means for those boys
who took both measures. However, all groups show similar patterns

of differences in peer aggression as a function of the experimental treatment. The control group peer aggression means are consistently higher than the experimental group means. In the case of aggression toward authority, the control and aggressive TV group means are about equal for subjects who took only the pretest. For the other two groups the control group means are higher. From these data it is evident that the overall differences in aggressive behavior between the experimental and control groups were not biased by differential participation in the experiment. As an additional check, separate analyses of the general peer aggression scores as a function of participation in the pretest and posttest were carried out for the boys' home and private school groups. These data are presented in Table 21. In order to have this table correspond to the previous one for the total sample, mean rather than median figures are given, although the means and medians are fairly close to each other. As one might anticipate, the differences in the private school population are negligible while in the boys' homes the aggressive TV group displays consistently less aggression than the controls. This is not surprising since most of the boys' homes subjects who took only one test participated in the project for at least five of the six weeks; fewer than ten dropped completely from the experiment.

Mean scores obtained in the initial personality measures and also on the instruments used to assess before-after changes in attitudes and values also were separately analyzed for those who took both tests and for those who took only the pretest. The data add little to the information on the attitude and value measures that have been previously presented and discussed. There is a significant difference in the group which took only the pretest in the sentence advocated for the delinquent. This difference occurs in the military academy, in which most of the change in subject population took place, and does not hold when the boys' homes are examined separately. Note has already been taken of the initial differences on the aggressive activity preference and peer nomination measures. The mean differences on the measures of overt and covert hostility, neurotic undercontrol, conflict, and aggression anxiety are small and are statistically insignificant. This is also the case when separate comparisons are made for the boys' homes and for the private

Table 21. AGGRESSION TOWARD PEERS AS A FUNCTION OF
EXPERIMENTAL TREATMENT, INSTITUTIONS, AND PARTICIPATION
IN THE PRETEST AND POSTTEST

			Boys' Homes	Private Schools
Subjects With Pretest Only	Control	Mean	4.45	.97
		N	(22)	(32)
	Agg. TV	Mean	1.68	.88
		N	(21)	(33)
		p	< .01	NS
Subjects With Posttest Only	Control	Mean	3.96	0.58
		N	(15)	(37)
	Agg. TV	Mean	1.86	0.21
		N	(14)	(37)
		p	< .05	NS
Subjects With Pre- and Posttests	Control	Mean	5.01	1.07
		N	(118)	(85)
	Agg. TV	Mean	2.69	1.10
		N	(116)	(76)
		p	< .0001	NS

schools. It appears reasonable to conclude that the experimental effect observed in the boys' homes cannot be attributed to selective differences between the aggressive TV and control groups in degree of participation in the experiment.

On the basis of other findings and preliminary interviews

before the experiment proper was undertaken, it was our impression that boys seemed to prefer TV programs with aggressive content to programs with nonaggressive content. The reports of personnel at the several institutions and our own observations during the study indicate that the difference in preference was not major and that the control subjects had the opportunity to see programs they enjoyed. The TV program reaction forms which the boys submitted provide data which directly bear on this issue. While this vast amount of data has not been analyzed in detail, the affective reactions to the programs have been tabulated and permit comparison between the responses of the control subjects to the nonaggressive TV programs and the responses of the experimental group to the aggressive TV diet. The subjects were asked to rate each program they watched on a six-point scale ranging from "liked it very much" to "disliked it very much." The aggressive TV group tended to rate their programs more positively than did the controls. However, the difference between the groups is small, a substantial majority of both sets of ratings falling in the positive categories. Thus 70 per cent of the control and 77 per cent of the aggressive TV programs were rated "liked it very much" or "liked it fairly much" while only 15 per cent of the control and 8 per cent of the aggressive TV programs received "dislike" ratings.

A list of affects was provided on the program rating sheet and the respondent was asked to indicate how strong his response to the program was by checking one of three alternatives: "not at all," "a little," and "very" for each of the ten feeling states listed. Although it must be kept in mind that, as with the like-dislike ratings, percentages are based on numbers of programs rather than numbers of people, the data are nonetheless informative. In regard to the ascription "bored," for example, the great majority of program ratings—80 per cent of the aggressive TV and 77 per cent of the controls—were "not at all"; the difference between the two sets of programs is quite small. While the aggressive and control TV programs elicited similar degrees of interest, the pattern of affective responses to these programs differs. Seventy-one per cent of the aggressive and 56 per cent of the control programs elicited ratings of "a little" or "very" excited. The aggressive TV programs also

tended to elicit higher percentages of such negative affective reactions as "afraid" (23 per cent aggressive TV and 6 per cent control), "annoyed" (18 per cent aggressive TV and 14 per cent
control), "nervous" (25 per cent aggressive TV and 7 per cent
control), "angry" (15 per cent aggressive TV and 8 per cent control), "sad" (22 per cent aggressive TV and 7 per cent control),
and "upset" (16 per cent aggressive TV and 9 per cent control).
In contrast, the control programs tended to elicit more positive
affective reactions; the percentages for "good" were 82 per cent
control and 78 per cent aggressive TV, and those for "happy," 62
per cent control and 40 per cent aggressive TV.

The greater number of program ratings in the control condition than in the aggressive TV condition does not necessarily indicate that the control group watched more television. Of the nonaggressive programs constituting the basic control diet, 23.6 per cent
are more than half an hour long; of the aggressive programs in the
basic diet 61.5 per cent are more than half an hour long. Using
these percentages to convert the approximately eight thousand control ratings and six thousand aggressive TV ratings into TV viewing
time yields estimates of 4,944 hours for the controls and 4,805
hours for the experimental group. These figures are very close, and,
while they represent indirect estimates, it seems likely that there is
no appreciable difference in the amount of television watched by the
controls and the aggressive TV group.

These data provide little support for the conjecture that
the control subjects were very dissatisfied with their program diet
and therefore reacted aggressively to peers and to authority figures.
They liked the great majority of programs they watched and found
most of them interesting. While these programs were less exciting
than the aggressive TV programs, they were also less distressing and
were more likely to elicit happy feelings.

Test-retest correlations for the combined experimental and
control groups and for each of these groups independently are presented in Table 22. Some of the correlations are surprisingly low,
particularly for the neurotic undercontrol, overt hostility, and covert
hostility measures, since these measures are based on factor-analyzed
scales. These correlations, however, tend to underestimate the re-

Table 22. Test-Retest Correlations

Measure	Control		Agg. TV		Total Sample
	r	N	r	N	r
Physical Aggression in Fantasy	.35	(203)	.42	(198)	.38
Intensity of Fantasy Aggression	.30	(207)	.42	(199)	.35
Aggressive Activity Preference	.61	(198)	.58	(189)	.61
Aggressive Values	.50	(175)	.54	(156)	.52
Peer Rating	.49	(114)	.46	(108)	.49
Aggression Anxiety	.51	(205)	.42	(195)	.46
Neurotic Undercontrol	.28	(206)	.34	(196)	.31
Overt Hostility	.46	(206)	.44	(197)	.45
Covert Hostility	.37	(205)	.42	(198)	.40
Conflict over Aggression	.38	(183)	.41	(168)	.40
Recommended Sentence	.29	(203)	.35	(192)	.32
Recommended Treatment	.47	(203)	.40	(192)	.44
Liking for Aggressive Shows	.46	(181)	.45	(167)	.46
Liking for Nonaggressive Shows	.48	(183)	.56	(168)	.52
Situation Test	.47	(152)	.50	(153)	.49

liabilities, since these variables may have been affected by the experimental treatment and by other factors that produced changes in these predispositions over time. Split-half correlations that have been reported for the measures of aggression anxiety, neurotic undercontrol, overt hostility, and covert hostility measures are all greater than .60 when corrected for attenuation. The fact that some of these correlations are greater than the test-retest correlations demonstrates that the latter are underestimates. We would have preferred higher reliabilities for the personality measures. For the dependent measures, very high reliabilities could reflect a lack of sensitivity to actual changes. However, the reliabilities are sufficiently high for the measures to be responsive to the experimental variable.

In interpreting some of our findings it may be helpful to review the correlations among the various measures used as reflected on the pretests. The correlation matrix in Table 23 is based on the entire sample, including the two nonparticipating comparison schools. The sample for the peer nomination measure is considerably less than those for the other variables since the peer nomination measure was administered only to the California schools. The nonparticipating schools also did not receive the fantasy measure. The correlations, although low, are still statistically significant due to the large sample, and they cluster into meaningful patterns. Overt hostility, covert hostility, and neurotic undercontrol are substantially related to each other and show similar relationships to other variables with one exception: Aggression anxiety is negatively correlated with overt hostility but is positively related to neurotic undercontrol and covert hostility. Evidence consistent with the psychological properties attributed to aggression anxiety is provided by its sizeable positive correlation with the conflict measure and its large negative correlations with aggressive activity preference, aggressive values, punitive attitudes toward the delinquent, and approval of aggressive alternatives on the situation test. Aggression anxiety and conflict over aggression are measures of the same construct and show similar relationships with other variables except for the positive correlation of conflict with overt hostility.

Subjects who are anxious or in conflict over aggression tend to prefer nonaggressive shows. The only variable correlating more

Table 23. CORRELATIONS OF PERSON

PAF	I	AA	NUC	OH	CH	C
Physical Agg. in Fantasy (PAF)	.74** (524)	— .01 (514)	.10* (517)	.11* (520)	.09* (521)	.01 (460)
Intensity of Fantasy Agg. (I)		— .02 (515)	.12** (518)	.14** (521)	.11* (522)	.04 (396)
Aggression Anxiety (AA)			.18** (748)	— .09* (751)	.29** (753)	.50** (688)
Neurotic Undercontrol (NUC)				.50** (753)	.55** (755)	.34** (685)
Overt Hostility (OH)					.41** (758)	.14** (687)
Covert Hostility (CH)						.41** (689)
Conflict (C)						
Agg. Activity Preference						
Aggressive Values						
Peer Nomination						
Recommended Sentence						
Recommended Treatment						
Situation Test						
Liking for Agg. Shows						

* p $<$ .05
** p $<$ .01

ALITY VARIABLES AND DEPENDENT MEASURES

Agg. Act. Pref.	Agg. Val.	Peer Nom.	Sent.	Treat.	Sit.	Liking Agg. Shows	Liking Nonagg. Shows
.10* (508)	.12* (474)	.12* (357)	.01 (508)	.07 (509)	.17** (449)	.08 (478)	.14** (480)
.09* (509)	.12* (475)	.14** (357)	.03 (509)	.08 (510)	.12* (450)	.11* (479)	.08 (481)
— .22** (731)	— .25** (696)	.04 (355)	—.03 (725)	— .15** (726)	— .24** (656)	— .03 (702)	.24** (704)
.12** (733)	.17** (698)	.17** (359)	— .02 (727)	.06 (728) q	.15** (657)	— .08* (705)	— .03 (707)
.17** (736)	.26** (701)	.16** (361)	— .01 (730)	.06 (731)	.21** (660)	— .06 (707)	— .12** (709)
.06 (738)	.14** (703)	.14* (362)	.01 (732)	.00 (733)	.15** (662)	— .01 (709)	.08* (711)
— .06 (670)	— .10* (636)	— .03 (307)	— .02 (661)	— .10* (662)	— .08 (598)	.00 (641)	.15** (643)
	.17** (695)	.14* (353)	— .01 (724)	.05 (725)	.25** (651)	.14** (695)	— .07 (697)
		.03 (317)	.07 (685)	.16** (686)	.38** (627)	— .02 (663)	— .10* (665)
			— .09 (355)	— .07 (355)	.21** (317)	.04 (350)	.10 (350)
				.45** (734)	— .12** (646)	.05 (690)	— .05 (692)
					.04 (647)	— .01 (691)	— .10* (693)
						.00 (623)	— .07 (625)
							.29** (711)

highly with liking of nonaggressive TV shows is liking of aggressive
TV shows, which suggests a general factor of TV preference. The
measures of fantasy aggression are also positively correlated with
liking of nonaggressive and aggressive shows. The two fantasy measures are highly correlated and appear to be functionally equivalent
in their relationship with other variables. Aggressive activity preference is also positively correlated with liking of aggressive shows while
boys high in overt hostility, aggressive values, and punitive treatment
of the delinquent tend to show a weaker preference for nonaggressive shows than low scorers on these variables.

The dependent measures of aggressive activity preference,
aggressive values, and peer nomination, and the situation test are
positively correlated and also relate positively to overt hostility,
covert hostility, and neurotic undercontrol. The peer nomination
measure is of special interest, since all the other measures are based on
the subject's own responses to questionnaires. The significant positive
although low correlations of peer nominations of aggression with
fantasy aggression and with the questionnaire measures of aggression
provide evidence of the concurrent validity of these measures.

A number of the personality and aggressive value measures
were administered to school children living at home in order to
provide some basis for estimating the degree of similarity between
the experimental population and a typical school population. Of the
measures administered to the comparison population—aggressive
values, situation test, aggressive activity preference, recommended
sentence, and like-dislike of nonaggressive and aggressive TV shows
—the comparison schools and experimental population differed significantly on one; the experimental groups obtained a significantly
higher mean score on the aggressive activity preference measure.
The means for the comparison schools are similar to those of the
experimental population on all the personality measures except the
conflict index for which the comparison school mean is significantly
lower than the experimental population mean. There is considerable
variation among the participating institutions in the mean scores on
this measure. Considering all the comparison school and experimental population means, it appears that the two populations are

quite similar, at least with respect to the particular measures used in this study.

The total control and aggressive group means are similar for overt hostility, covert hostility, aggression anxiety, and conflict while the aggressive TV group tends to have higher scores on the neurotic undercontrol measure $(p < .10)$. This difference occurs largely at Pacific Lodge Home. In view of a similar difference on the aggressive activity preference test, it appears that due to chance or reasons unknown to us, the aggressive TV group in this institution was initially more aggressive than the controls. This initial difference renders the greater behavior aggression ratings displayed by the controls than by the aggressive TV group in this institution all the more striking. In general, the controls and aggressive TV group were initially similar on the pretests and the few differences found showed greater initial aggressiveness in the aggressive TV group.

EIGHT

Conclusions

The experimental results are, on the whole, consistent, and some of the findings, particularly those bearing on the acting out of aggression, are striking. The most modest conclusion we can make from the data is that exposure to aggressive content in television over a six-week period does not produce an increment in aggressive behavior. The only measure on which the controls decreased relative to the aggressive TV group was fantasy aggression. About all one can state regarding this latter finding is that boys who witness mostly nonaggressive content in television make up fewer stories in which fighting takes place than boys who watch a great deal of fighting on television. The results, in fact, indicate that witnessing aggressive TV programs reduces rather than stimulates the acting out of aggressive tendencies in certain types of boys.

140

This generalization requires qualification, particularly in regard to the populations to which it applies. The effect is pronounced in children with certain personality and social characteristics and is weak or absent in other personality constellations. We need also to examine the conditions of the experiment and consider possible alternate explanations of the findings. Nevertheless, what is most compelling about the data is the regularity with which the obtained differences in aggressive behaviors and changes in aggressive attitudes and values point to a reducing or controlling rather than to a stimulating or disinhibiting effect of exposure to aggressive interaction in television programs.

Since a fairly detailed analysis of the data was undertaken and since there are exceptions to the overall generalization, a brief review of the specific findings may be helpful: Boys exposed to aggressive TV content manifested significantly less behavioral aggression toward peers and authority than boys exposed to nonaggressive TV content. For convenience, this finding will be referred to as the experimental effect. The experimental effect holds only for residents of the boys' homes, there being little difference in aggression toward peers and toward authority between control and aggressive TV groups in the private schools. Among the boys' home residents, the aggressive TV group manifested less physical and verbal aggression toward peers than did the controls. There were also highly reliable differences between the controls and the aggressive TV groups in physical and verbal aggression toward authority. The trend analysis revealed a significant decline in authority aggression in boys' home residents exposed to the aggressive diet, the difference in linear trend between the aggressive TV and control groups being highly reliable for the verbal aggression toward authority factor. There was a large initial difference on the verbal aggression toward peers factor between the aggressive TV and control groups. Although the difference is not statistically reliable (at the .05 level) and may in part reflect the influence of the experimental treatment, it could have affected the findings for this factor. However, when the population was divided into three groups on the basis of their initial peer aggression scores, the experimental effect was still obtained on at least one behavior dimension for each of the three levels of aggression.

Age does not appear to be an important variable, although
the most reliable experimental effects for the boys' home sample
were obtained for high school students and the next most reliable
for elementary school students. The differences between the aggressive TV and control groups for the junior high sample are in the
same direction as the other comparisons but are not statistically reliable. Of particular interest is the suggested reversal of the experimental effect in the private school sample for junior high school
boys on the physical aggression toward authority factor. In view
of the overwhelming number of nonsignificant findings obtained
for the private school sample, it is reasonable to attribute to chance
such occasional evidence of a significant difference. Nevertheless,
because of the social implications of these results, special attention
should be given to deviant findings. Within the boys' home population, the experimental effect is strongest for boys high in overt and
covert hostility, high in peer nomination for aggression, high in
neurotic undercontrol, and low in aggression anxiety. That is, exposure to aggressive content in television produces a decrement in
aggression relative to exposure to nonaggressive television in boys
who have strong aggressive tendencies coupled with weak inhibitory
and ego controls. The one exception to this pattern is fantasy aggression, boys below the median in fantasy aggression being most
reliably and strongly affected by exposure to the aggressive or the
control diet. In both boys' home and private school samples, the
controls manifested a significantly greater increase in aggressive
values than did the aggressive TV groups for boys high in overt
hostility and high in peer aggression nominations. When personality
factors are not taken into account, the differences between the aggressive TV and control groups are insignificant.

In both boys' home and private school samples, the controls
manifested a significantly greater increase in aggressive options on
the situation test than did the aggressive TV group. These data
suggest that at least some boys in the private schools displayed a
response to the experimental treatment similar to that of the boys'
home residents. Again, the experimental effect measure is strongest
for subjects high in peer nominations of aggression. Also, the increment in the control group is significantly greater than the increment

in the aggressive TV group in boys high in aggression anxiety and in boys low in fantasy aggression. No significant differences between the aggressive TV and control groups were found on the aggressive activity preference measure. Differences in changes in severity of sentence advocated for a delinquent were small but in a direction consistent with the other experimental findings. When personality variables are taken into account, the control mean increment tends to be greater than the aggressive TV mean increment for boys high in neurotic undercontrol, low in overt hostility, high in covert hostility, and low in fantasy aggression. Significant differences between aggressive TV and control groups on the peer nomination of aggression measure were obtained only for some personality groups. Reliably greater increments in peer nominations for aggression in the controls than in the aggressive TV group were manifested in the low aggression anxiety, high fantasy aggression subsample in the boys' homes. A similar effect was obtained for low overt hostility boys for the combined boys' homes and private school population.

In contrast to the changes shown on the other dependent measures, the controls manifested a significantly greater decrement in fantasy aggression than did the aggressive TV group. The trends were similar for both boys' homes and private schools, the differences being most pronounced in boys above the median for several of the initial measures of aggressive disposition. Responses to the viewing habits measure, administered at the beginning and conclusion of the experiment, on which participants expressed their degree of liking for six TV shows with aggressive content and six programs with primarily nonaggressive content, indicated preference for aggressive programs, although nonaggressive programs were also liked. In addition, the boys' home controls showed an increase in liking of this selected sample of nonaggressive shows following their experimental experience. This effect is strongest for boys who were initially above the median on the peer nomination measure of aggression. The experimental variation in TV diet had little effect on the behavior rating scores of children in boys' homes who were initially high in fantasy aggression and low in overt hostility, but tended to produce strong differences in boys low in fantasy aggression and high in overt hostility. The findings were very similar when the peer aggression nomination index instead of the overt hostility questionnaire was used as the measure of manifest aggressive tendencies. However, private school boys who were initially high in fantasy aggression and high in peer aggression nominations displayed significantly more verbal aggression toward authority figures when exposed to aggressive content in television than when exposed to nonaggressive content. Significant differences were not obtained on other behavior comparisons for this personality subgroup. In addition opposite effects were obtained on some of the before-after change score measures, suggesting again that the occasional finding of a significant effect in the private schools is a chance effect.

Using responses to the list of six aggressive and six nonaggressive TV shows to establish initial frequency of TV viewing, we found that the experimental differences in the behavior rating scores were at least as strong for those boys in the boys' homes who had watched relatively little television as for those boys who were average or high in the frequency with which they had viewed TV before initiation of the experiment. Ratings submitted for the programs viewed indicated that both the control and aggressive TV subjects liked a substantial majority of the programs they observed.

The interpretation of these findings is constrained by the particular methodological approach which was taken in investigating the effects of violence in television and by cultural variables which characterize the population from which the experimental samples were drawn. In the design of this study, it was decided to use as experimental materials standard television fare rather than specially constructed or selected programs. In so doing, we sacrificed control of the structure, format, and precise content of the experimental stimuli but gained in representativeness and the extent to which the findings can be generalized to the kinds of programs that are presented on television. This generalization also implies a restriction. The aggressive content which the boys witnessed by no means encompassed the full range of violence and brutality that it is possible to depict on film or videotape. It may be that programs in which particular forms of aggression and brutality are rampant and are reinforced would have different effects than the programs observed by the aggressive TV group. These data apply only to the aggressive material that is portrayed on television in this country, or, to be more specific in southern California and greater New York.

Generalization about the effects of these programs is further limited by the six-week duration of the experiment. A longer period could conceivably have resulted in the elimination of differences between the experimental and control groups and perhaps even in a reversal of trends. This latter possibility seems most unlikely. There are no indications of a trend which if extrapolated would result in the aggressive TV group manifesting more aggression than the control group did. A longer duration might exaggerate the differences between the experimental and control groups and would very likely produce boredom and indifference in both. The question of the effects of the length of duration of the experimental period is a different question from that of the length of time to which children in this culture are exposed to violence on television. Our experimental sample was drawn from a population that has had a history of exposure to television and to other mass media. We began with boys who had already been conditioned by their society and then considered the behavioral consequences of systematic variation of their subsequent experiences. How this experimental variation would influence children from a different culture or children who have never been previously exposed to television or films or preschool and primary grade children are questions to which the present study was not addressed.

Within the restrictions of sample characteristics, range of stimuli utilized, and duration of the experiment, two major conclusions are indicated by the experimental findings: First, exposure to aggressive content in television does not lead to an increase in aggressive behavior. Second, exposure to aggressive content in television seems to reduce or control the expression of aggression in aggressive boys from relatively low socioeconomic backgrounds.

The first conclusion is a weaker inference than the second. Although a negative assertion or statement of no difference tends to have little theoretical import, its applied or social implications may have considerable significance. The major question that arises in evaluating any such assertion is methodological, particularly in regard to the reliability of the measures, their sensitivity to changes, and the degree in which the laboratory procedure relates to the real life phenomena of interest. The measures employed were in fact sufficiently reliable and sensitive to record significant effects of the experimental treatment. As for the degree to which the experiment reflects normal phenomena, a salient feature of the experimental design was the degree of representativeness achieved by incorporating experimental control into a field setting. The manipulation of aggressive content was accomplished by controlling exposure to regular television programs. The effectiveness of this controlled variation is reflected by the fact that the great majority of programs which each group watched were in accord with their experimental assignment. The import of the observed changes in aggression can be questioned in view of the gap between aggressive action and the measures of aggressive value and aggressive fantasy, although the latter are still of great interest. However, the ratings of peer and authority aggression were addressed to precisely the kinds of behaviors which are of social concern.

These features of the present experiment distinguish it from laboratory studies which have dealt with the same issues. The laboratory studies have yielded different outcomes depending on the aggressive content manipulated, the emotional state of the subjcts at the time the experimental stimuli were witnessed, and the particular measures used to evaluate the experimental effects. These studies have been intensively reviewed and critically evaluated by Hartley (1964), and theoretical issues germane to the frequently conflicting results have been considered elsewhere (Feshbach, 1964, 1970).

Inasmuch as the President's Commission on Violence has asserted that aggression on television stimulates aggression in children, it may be useful to consider some of the sources of conflicting results and to reconcile opposing findings. The details of the Commission's report are not yet available to the authors, but the information on which the report is based is public and familiar to scholars concerned with this problem. We return to this question after an examination of the methodology and implications of the present experiment.

The second major conclusion, that witnessing aggressive content on TV reduces or regulates the expression of aggression, while supported by the data, may be objected to because of a design problem. We recognized from the very beginning of the study that boys preferred aggressive TV programs to nonaggressive programs, and we were concerned about the possibility that boys might resent being assigned to the nonaggressive diet. We were also concerned that there might be resistance to participation in the experiment regardless of diet. To enhance the attractiveness of the study to the boys and to engage their interest, we used volunteers whenever possible. Also, we met with the boys and reviewed the experimental procedures with them; their response was, for the most part, favorable and gratifying. In addition, except at the Military Academy, we offered each boy ten dollars for his participation. The boys were pleased by the prospect of receiving this money and were also pleased by the fact that new large-screen television sets were placed in their dormitories, cottages, or schoolrooms. (At the Ojai school we arranged to extend a TV cable to school facilities from which TV had previously been absent.) Finally, we maintained continuous contact with the participating institutions, and when an occasional problem arose, as when boys in the control group wished to see "Batman," we resolved it in favor of minimizing frustration. (In terms of the design, it was only essential that most but not necessarily all the programs watched be from the assigned diet. This objective was achieved.)

The responses of the boys to the TV programs they watched provide further evidence that the control condition was not frustrating. The boys in this group liked most of the programs they saw, and the difference between the controls and aggressive TV groups in the proportion of programs disliked is small, 15 per cent compared to 8 per cent. The affective responses to the programs also reflected generally positive reactions by the controls to the programs in their diet. Although their implications are indirect, the data based on the like-dislike ratings of the list of six aggressive and six nonaggressive programs in the pretest and posttest are also of some relevance. While the mean ratings for the six nonaggressive programs were lower than the means for the aggressive programs, at the four boys' homes, where the controls displayed significantly greater peer aggression than the aggressive TV group, the initial mean rating for the nonaggressive programs was already high; at two other institutions the controls showed significant increments in their mean ratings after the six-week exposure period. Also, the positive correlation between liking of aggressive programs and liking of nonaggressive programs was considerably higher than the correlation between the like-dislike ratings and the personality measures. Finally, the correlations of the like-dislike ratings for the aggressive programs and nonaggressive programs with peer and authority aggression were separately examined for the control and aggressive TV groups and in all instances were insignificantly different from zero.

Other data discount the hypothesis that the experimental effects are due to frustration experienced by the controls at being placed on the nonaggressive diet. In regard to the like-dislike changes, for example, the private school controls appeared to be less enamored of the nonaggressive diet after exposure to it, yet there was no evidence of an increase in aggression in this group compared to the private school aggressive TV group. The rare significant differences that were found in behavior ratings for the private school sample reflected, in fact, less aggression in the controls than in the aggressive TV group. The fact that in the boys' home sample the aggressive TV group displayed significantly less behavioral aggression than the controls even for boys who had been relatively infrequent observers of television is a further argument against a frustration hypothesis. If the assignment of boys to the nonaggressive diet constituted a frustration of their ordinary viewing habits, then the high frequency TV viewer should show the strongest experimental effect. There are no indications from these data of differential resentment. While the hypothesis that resentment was elicited and was sufficient to partly account for the differences in peer and authority aggression and the differential changes in the aggressive value measures cannot be completely discounted, the data indicate that the hypothesis is highly improbable.

Since so many of the key findings are based on the behavior ratings, some additional comment on the ratings and raters is appropriate. Perhaps the most salient aspect of the ratings is their variability. There was considerable day-to-day and week-to-week variation in aggression ratings for a particular child or for a particular cottage and also considerable variation among raters. Nevertheless, when assessed over several weeks, the behavior ratings for aggression proved to be systematically related to a number of other variables; for example, boys obtaining high aggression scores on the behavior ratings also tended to obtain high aggression scores on the peer nomination index. As for rater variability and its possible effects on the data, when the means for each rater who rated both aggressive TV and control groups were used as the unit of comparison, significant differences between the aggressive TV and the control groups were still obtained. Also relevant is the consistency of the major experimental trends across all four of the boys' homes.

The question of possible systematic biases in the ratings remains. While most cottage parents and supervisors did not appear to be aware of the major purpose of the experiment, we cannot discount the possibility that there was some awareness but not at a sufficient level to permit verbalization of the experimental contingency. Still, when, during preliminary contacts with the various institutions, opinions were volunteered concerning the influence of television on boys, the catharsis hypothesis rarely appeared. Most people felt either that violence on television had little influence or that it tended to stimulate aggressive behavior. Thus, if rater biases were a factor they would tend to influence the outcome in an opposite direction to that actually found.

An equally important consideration is the systematic relationship between the experimental differences obtained and the personality characteristics of the boys who participated in the study. The fact that the experimental differences were most pronounced for those boys in the boys' home sample who were initially high in overt aggression and low in fantasy makes it quite improbable that rater bias influenced the ratings of the controls and of the aggressive TV group in any regular manner. To produce such an outcome would require rather complex cognitive discriminations on the part of the raters, as well as a hypothesis concerning the impact of aggression in television which few seemed to entertain.

We turn now to a consideration of possible mechanisms

mediating the effects of exposure to aggressive and nonaggressive TV content. One possibility, but to us an unlikely one, is that the situation comedies seen as part of the nonaggressive diet tend to reduce restraint and thereby increase aggressive and other behaviors which are normally inhibited. Why this process should result in an increase on the cognitive measures of aggressive value is unclear to us. More germane, however, is the fact that a number of the aggressive programs were also of this type—for example "Man from Uncle" and "Get Smart." Moreover, a primary characteristic of the aggressive shows is reduced restraint in connection with the expression of aggression. This ready expression of aggression is more specific and salient than the reduction of inhibition sometimes depicted in the situation comedies. Of course, aggression as depicted in the aggressive TV shows is frequently followed by punishment, a sequence which may foster inhibition of aggressive expression. Reactions to the aggressive shows indicate that negative affects were elicited, which may have had an inhibitory function. Increased inhibition of aggression would account for the tendency of the aggressive TV group in those institutions showing an experimental effect to decline in peer aggression over the six-week period, but cannot satisfactorily account for the increments in the controls on the change measures. Since these changes are at best relative, this objection is by no means crucial.

Because we did not attempt to control the stimulus properties of the TV programs within a particular diet, we cannot exclude the possibility that factors associated with aggressive and nonaggressive content may be responsible for the observed changes or may contribute, along with the variations in exposure to aggressive content, to the experimental effects. However, the pattern of experimental findings, particularly of the personality correlates of the experimental effects, points to a theoretical interpretation which focuses on the functional significance of fantasy behavior and the status of television viewing as a fantasy experience.

In the initial formulation of this project, the TAT-type measure of aggression was conceived of as an index of aggressive drive. It was assumed that the stories constructed by the subjects in response to the pictures shown them would be particularly sensitive to covert aggressive tendencies and would be a more valid indicator of aggressive motivation than the questionnaire and sociometric procedures. The questionnaire and sociometric procedures were assumed to be more valid indicators of manifest aggressive behavior tendencies which, while influenced by aggressive drive, are also influenced by inhibitory factors and the availability of the aggressive responses in the child's behavioral repertoire. Many psychologists, particularly Skinnerians and positivists, would take issue with this effort to distinguish between aggressive drive and aggressive behavior and between latent and overt aggressive tendencies. We also would now modify the above formulations but on different grounds.

The conceptualization of the TAT as a projective technique which is sensitive to subtle variations in human motivations has a long history beginning with the initial development of the technique (Murray, 1938). The TAT has been used extensively by clinicians as a measure of motivation. Also, a rather large experimental literature documents the sensitivity of TAT stories to experimentally induced motivational changes (McClelland and others, 1953; Murstein, 1965; Zubin, Eron, and Shumer, 1965). In addition, both experimentalists and clinicians have contributed to the development of specific scoring systems for assessing such diverse motivations as achievement, aggression, affiliation, sex, dependency, anxiety, and power. Interest has been focused on the strength of particular motivational tendencies, on the situations which appear to stimulate these motivations, and on the modes of response to these motivations.

The relationship between measures of motivational tendencies as reflected in TAT stories and overt behavioral manifestations of motive has been explored in an extensive number of studies. (For a summary of the literature on the relationship between children's aggressive behavior and TAT aggression, see Feshbach, 1970.) The general issue to which most studies have been addressed is whether TAT story themes represent actual behavioral expressions or serve as a compensation or substitute for an inhibited motivational tendency. In either case the TAT response is seen as an indicator of the strength of some motivational tendency.

The compensation hypothesis can be divided into two em-

pirically distinct issues. One question pertains to the relationship
between fantasy aggression and overt aggression. The other concerns
the functional value of fantasy aggression. For example, children
who have a great deal of aggression anxiety and tend to inhibit overt
aggressive behaviors may display more TAT fantasy aggression
than children who are freer in overt aggressive expressions, although
this relationship has not been fully demonstrated. However, evidence
of an inverse relationship between overt and fantasy aggression
would not be evidence that TAT fantasy serves as an outlet or safety
valve for pent up aggressive impulses. Kurt Lewin's distinction between substitute valence and substitute value is relevant here. An
activity may be highly attractive (have high valence) following
frustration or inhibition but may have little value in reducing
frustration. More direct data bearing on the motivational functions
of fantasy activity are required to demonstrate its discharge, or substitute value, function.

The properties of the TAT are relevant to the present study
in two respects. They bear on the interpretation of the greater experimental effect obtained for boys low in fantasy aggression. Moreover, many considerations regarding TAT fantasy are also applicable to the observations of violence on television. TAT fantasy responses are seen as being basically on the same continuum as overt
aggressive tendencies, the principal issue being the role of inhibition
in determining the intensity of these responses and a second issue
being the cathartic value of this fantasied aggressive content. These
conceptions of TAT fantasy generally ignore the cognitive aspects
of the fantasy activity. When a child is engaging in TAT fantasy
aggression, he is manipulating verbal symbols, drawing upon his
imaginative resources, and otherwise engaging in a complex cognitive act. The implications of the cognitive aspects of TAT fantasy
should be distinguished from their motivational attributes.

The psychological connection and difference between fantasy behavior and real behavior needs to be understood in terms
of the particular psychological processes that mediate each form of
behavior. There is considerable evidence that the cognitive activity
of fantasy, in thoughts, dreams, stories, or reveries, enables the child
or adult to delay and control the immediate expression of impulses.

This proposition, initially formulated by Freud, has been expanded and applied by psychoanalytic ego psychology to a wide variety of phenomena. As a recent monograph on daydreaming states, "The adolescent who cannot provide himself pleasure through internal fantasy, contemplation, or manipulation of daydream images is compelled more directly to an overt motor imitation of the adult pattern" (Singer, 1966, p. 176). There are obvious differences among daydreaming, TAT fantasy, and fantasies presented through the mass media. The media can stimulate imitation, which is not true of self-generated fantasies. At the same time, dramatic content in television and in other media are also fantasies, a point which has not been adequately considered in research and theory on media effects.

There may be a functional equivalence between some of the processes in the generation of a TAT story with aggressive content and in the more passive exposure to aggressive content in the media. They are both cognitive activities, they are both concerned with "unreal" elements, and, we argue, they both may help mitigate the instigation to action. The present findings may fruitfully be viewed in this context.

The experimental results that require interpretation and integration may be briefly summarized: Assignment to the aggressive TV diet resulted in significantly fewer aggressive attitudes and less aggressive behavior than did assignment to the control diet. This effect was pronounced in the boys' homes and did not occur in the private schools. The preponderance of comparisons in the private school sample was statistically insignificant, and the few significant differences obtained were inconsistent. The experimental effect was particularly pronounced in boys with strong manifest aggressive tendencies. The experimental effect was more pronounced in boys initially low in TAT fantasy aggression than in boys high in fantasy aggression.

If one attributes a cognitive control function to aggressive fantasy including the vicarious imaginative activity entailed in observing aggressive content on television, then assignment to the aggressive TV diet provides an opportunity for extensive cognitive supports and, excluding the effects of other processes, a decrement in the acting out of aggressive tendencies can be anticipated. Placing boys on the control diet removes the cognitive support provided by vicarious aggressive fantasy, resulting in an exaggeration or release of aggressive behaviors. This process has the quality of a deprivation or withdrawal experience and is reminiscent of the effects of dream deprivation on subsequent dreaming. One can further anticipate that these effects are stronger in boys who have fewer internal cognitive resources and are therefore more dependent on external cognitive supports for control of their aggressive impulses.

The private school and boys' home boys differ in cognitive resources. The private school boys have higher IQ scores, a greater number are college-oriented, and they are likely to read more than the boys' home residents. Reading could be considered an external rather than an internal cognitive activity. However, the relevant differentiation is the relative involvement in reading and in watching television. It is assumed that children who read a great deal have less need for the cognitive supports that observation of television can provide than do children who read little. The data reported by Schramm, Lyle, and Parker (1961) regarding the inverse relationship between the amount of reading and the degree of exposure to other media is consistent with this hypothesis. Their findings suggest that there is an almost fixed amount of time, possibly reflecting a stable need, which children devote to the mass media. If more time is spent with one communication medium, less time is spent with another. We are tempted to infer that these relationships hold for specific media content so that exposure to aggressive content in one medium reduces the necessity for exposure to such content in other media.

We suggest that the boys' home residents are more dependent on aggressive TV content for behavior control than are the private school students. This interpretation is admittedly made after the fact, and a great many other differences between the private schools and boys' homes could be responsible for the difference in response to the experimental treatment. The settings were very different, the private school group may have been more sophisticated about the purposes and procedures of the experiment, and they tended to be less interested and less cooperative. For these reasons, one has to be especially cautious in attributing the absence of an overall experimental effect in the private school sample to their greater cognitive resources. In addition, the occasional reversals in trends found in this group, while probably chance occurrences, reinforce the necessity for caution in interpreting the private school data.

The relationship of the personality variables to the experimental effects provides the most cogent basis for the cognitive support interpretation of the experimental differences obtained in the boys' home groups. A highly consistent finding was that larger experimental differences were obtained in boys who were initially highly aggressive. These boys presumably have a greater need for cognitive controls than less aggressive youngsters do. The highly aggressive boy placed on the control diet was deprived of a particularly needed cognitive support, while the same boy assigned to the aggressive TV diet was provided with additional opportunities for vicarious aggressive fantasy.

The association of low fantasy aggression with the experimental effect is also consistent with this interpretation. The results of the analysis of the high and low physical aggression in fantasy personality groupings, while not as uniform as those obtained for the manifest aggression measures, generally reflect a stronger experimental effect in boys who were below the median in aggressive fantasy. This finding is particularly intriguing since it deviates from the pattern obtained for the manifest aggression variables, which, in addition, are positively correlated with fantasy aggression. It suggests that the boy who does not or cannot engage in self-generated aggressive fantasy needs the external support provided by the vicarious fantasy experience of watching violence on television. In contrast to the high manifest aggression boys whose "need" for cognitive support stems from the strength of their aggressive tendencies, the "need" of the low fantasy subjects stems from their lack of adequate cognitive resources. This would especially be the case for low fantasy aggression boys with strong manifest aggressive tendencies, and, indeed, the experimental effects tend to be strongest for this group.

The cognitive support interpretation is very similar to the catharsis hypothesis, and the catharsis hypothesis is also consistent with much of the data. The possibility that observations of violence on television may partially reduce aggressive drive is operationally difficult to separate from the coping function, which has been attributed to aggressive fantasy, whether self-generated or vicariously observed. Nevertheless, we favor the cognitive support hypothesis for several reasons. It accounts for the lack of findings in the private school sample better than the catharsis hypothesis does. It also is more consonant with the TAT story findings, although the catharsis hypothesis, with some awkwardness, can also account for these data. Perhaps most compelling from a theoretical viewpoint is that the cognitive structure hypothesis is in greater accord with current conceptions of the functions of fantasy and related ego processes.

Possibly both functions of aggressive fantasy—control of impulses and drive discharge—are operating. Observation of aggression on television may offer an already hostile and angry viewer an opportunity to vicariously express his feelings and thus offer some form of satisfaction. A subtle but useful distinction can be made between emotional expression and drive satisfaction (Feshbach, 1964). Witnessing violence portrayed on television may not satisfy desires to inflict injury on particular peers or authority figures but may permit the vicarious expression of angry feelings. From this point of view, the particular aggressive acts that are depicted and the resultant inflicted injuries and successes achieved by the violence are secondary to the affective concomitants of the action. The term *catharsis* should probably be restricted to its original meaning of an emotional cleansing. The dramatic arts, in that sense, may help purge the audience's feelings without eliminating sources of frustration or may even provide substitutes for motivated aggressive behavior. Some such process could be occurring along wtih the posited cognitive control function of fantasy.

For either of these processes to operate, it is essential that the subject already be angry and aggressive. There must be some impulse to control or cathart. In addition, one would not expect the depiction of aggression to have a stimulating effect on boys who are already manifestly aggressive. Similarly, modeling effects are less relevant for these boys since they have already acquired a repertoire of aggressive behavior. In brief, they have little to learn in the way of aggression and are not very inhibited in responding aggressively. The absence of a stimulation effect in these boys from exposure to the aggressive TV diet is not surprising. The absence of an increment in aggression in the boys who are more inhibited and in the boys with weaker aggressive tendencies is somewhat surprising although not inconsistent with the empirical literature. Evidence of stimulation effects of modeling has been obtained primarily from restricted laboratory studies since field investigations generally yield indifferent outcomes concerning the effects of violence on the aggressive behavior of the audience.

We have previously considered those aspects of the present investigation which distinguish it from other field studies as well as from laboratory experiments. In view of the radical differences in procedures and in variables examined between this experimental field study and others, there is no problem in reconciling the evidence obtained here of a control or cathartic property of exposure to aggressive content with the data obtained in other field investigations. At the same time, replication of the present findings under a variety of conditions and with other populations would be requisite to any conclusion that exposure to aggressive content in television helps control acting out tendencies in highly aggressive boys. Certainly, the present data point in that direction, and, in addition, the findings form a theoretically coherent pattern. However, no single experiment is ever decisive and there may be special conditions operating in the settings we selected which limit the generalizability of the findings that viewing aggressive TV reduces aggressive behavior while viewing nonaggressive TV enhances aggression.

We are, however, willing to conclude that the kind of aggressive television content to which most American preadolescent and adolescent boys are exposed does not stimulate aggressive behavior in working class boys, and we believe the same to be true for middle-class boys, although we recognize the occasional suggestion of a stimulating effect in some private school subgroups. We searched extensively for indications of aggression enhancement and did not find them. The absence of significant aggression enhancement effects resulting from exposure to aggressive content in television cannot be attributed to our measures. They were sufficiently reliable to yield consistent evidence of aggression control effects resulting from witnessing violent action sequences on television. One reason for the absence of aggression stimulation is that although laboratory situations may have features which communicate to the subject that it is permissible to behave aggressively, under more typical viewing circumstances, the television programs are perceived as having little relevance to social behavior; that is, the programs are perceived as fantasy, as fictional, and as unreal. What is appropriate to fiction need not be seen as appropriate to reality.

We suggest that there are sharp differences in responses to fantasy content and to reality content and that the message of fantasy is much less influential in shaping children's aggressive attitudes than the message of reality. Most children, except the very young and the seriously emotionally disturbed, are quite capable of distinguishing fantasy from reality (Himmelweit, 1958). This discrimination of stimuli is reflected in discriminable differences in responses. The child's individual learning experiences and typical socialization practices tend to reinforce a different set of responses to fantasy than to reality expressions. A mother may respond with amusement to the sight of one child playfully burying another on the beach sands. Her response (and that of the youngster playing dead) would not be one of amusement if this interaction was actually being enacted.

We suggest that violence presented in the form of fiction is much less likely to reinforce, stimulate, or elicit aggressive responses in children than is violence in the form of a news event. This is not to say that fictional material does not have instructional value or does not elicit incidental learning. But, we argue, the world of drama, play, and imagination is not the same as the world of daily social interaction, work, and factual communication. Yet much of the experimental literature on the effects of exposure to violence seems to treat dramatic forms as if they were equivalent to real events or to direct interaction. It is a moot question whether there is a higher proportion of thieves and other antisocial deviants among children who have read *Treasure Island* or who have seen the pirates of the Barbary Coast extolled and romanticized in film than among other children.

Social scientists have not only tended to treat fictional forms as if they were fundamentally equivalent to nonfiction but have also ignored important psychological dimensions basic to the impact of a fictional experience. We refer specifically to the esthetic aspects of fictional communication. Surely the esthetic dimensions of a television drama with aggressive sequences have some bearing on what is communicated to the child. Drama critics since Aristotle, in analyzing the impact of a play, have been as much concerned with its structure as with its content. Language style, denouement, and other elements that contribute to the esthetic experience are the grist for their critical analysis. Psychologists have not yet developed concepts and methods for evaluating the role of the esthetic dimension in determining the impact of a violent display, yet its importance is obvious.

We wonder whether some of the concern regarding the effects of the depiction of violence on television on at least the older child has not been misplaced. We assume that the techniques of presentation will remain similar to those currently used on television and will not take on the realism of films, where little is left to the imagination. The more realistic the technique, the more difficult it is for the child to perceive the display as fictional. Under these circumstances, our theoretical propositions concerning fantasy would not apply. The impact of a film employing a highly realistic mode of presentation is likely to be quite different from the impact of violence in fictional drama as currently presented. Systematic investigation of these possible differences ought to be undertaken.

However, given the current state of television fare, educators, child psychologists, and other professionals with an interest in children's welfare might more fruitfully direct their attention to the quality of television programs observed by children than to the aggressive content of the programs. The esthetic quality of programs aimed at young children and adolescents is appalling; programs are even inferior to adult fare. All too few programs capture and stimulate the child's imagination, provide the child with heroic models who enlist and strengthen his ideals, provide him with insight into his physical and social world, present a form and structure which enrich the child's sensibility as well as illuminate his experience. We suspect that if television fare equivalent to such violent epics as *Macbeth, Medea,* or *Treasure Island* were substituted for "The Untouchables," "Combat," and similar programs, there would be much less concern about the depiction of violence on television.

Appendices

A

Behavior
Rating Scale

Behavior Rating Scale

	Toward Peer				Toward Authority			
	Provoked		Unprovoked		Provoked		Unprovoked	
	Mild	Mod-Strong	Mild	Mod-Strong	Mild	Mod-Strong	Mild	Mod-Strong
1. Was in a fist fight, hit or kicked somebody.	——	——	——	——	——	——	——	——
2. Pushed or shoved someone.	——	——	——	——	——	——	——	——
3. Angry interchange or verbal blowup with someone.	——	——	——	——	——	——	——	——
4. Cursed someone, used profanity.	——	——	——	——	——	——	——	——
5. Made negative, critical or insulting remarks toward someone.	——	——	——	——	——	——	——	——
6. Expression of anger or criticism toward someone not present.	——	——	——	——	——	——	——	——
7. Was grumbling or generally complaining.	——	——	——	——	——	——	——	——
8. Was rough, careless or destroyed some property.	——	——	——	——	——	——	——	——
9. Had a particularly frustrating or unhappy experience.	——	——	——	——	——	——	——	——

10. Upset when criticized or corrected.	10.							
11. Avoiding people today.	11.							
12. Seemed unhappy.	12.							
13. Very bossy.	13.							
14. Bragged or boasted a lot.	14.							
15. Blaming others for problems.	15.							
16. Picking on or teasing others.	16.							
17. Was picked on today.	17.							
18. Broke a major rule.	18.							
19. Seemed to be trying to start trouble.	19.							
20. Angry or sullen facial expression.	20.							
21. Seemed to be jealous.	21.							
22. Was especially helpful.	22.							
23. Refused to perform voluntary or assigned tasks.	23.						
24. Threw object at someone or hurt someone through a "prank."	24.						
25. Was overly critical of himself.	25.							
26. Pounded his fist or otherwise hurt himself.	26.						

B

Supplementary Tables

Table B-1. PHYSICAL AGGRESSION TOWARD PEERS

BOYS' HOMES

	N	Overall Medians	Week-by-Week Medians							Linear Trends
			1	2	3	4	5	6	7	
Control	135	1.60	1.23	.85	.83	1.15	.97	1.70	1.96	+ **
Agg. TV	138	1.19	1.10	.79	1.49	.49	.67	.76	.77	− **
p of diff.		< .02	NS							< .002

PRIVATE SCHOOLS

	N	Overall Medians	Week-by-Week Medians							Linear Trends
			1	2	3	4	5	6	7	
Control	159	.18	.13	.08	.10	.10	.10	.10	.10	− *
Agg. TV	167	.22	.05	.05	.11	.12	.11	.11	.12	NS
p of diff.		NS								NS

Table B-2. Verbal Aggression Toward Peers

BOYS' HOMES

	N	Overall Medians	Week-by-Week Medians							Linear Trends
			1	2	3	4	5	6	7	
Control	135	2.42	2.18	1.53	1.73	1.52	1.57	2.44	2.47	NS
Agg. TV	138	1.09	1.04	.87	1.15	.67	.75	.60	.87	—**
p of diff.		<.04								<.06

PRIVATE SCHOOLS

	N	Overall Medians	Week-by-Week Medians							Linear Trends
			1	2	3	4	5	6	7	
Control	159	.51	.38	.43	.27	.49	.40	.10	.19	—
Agg. TV	166	.47	.09	.19	.34	.20	.28	.18	.17	NS
p of diff.		NS	NS							NS

Table B-3. Physical Aggression Toward Authority

BOYS' HOMES

| | N | Overall Medians | Week-by-Week Medians | | | | | | | Linear Trends |
			1	2	3	4	5	6	7	
Control	135	.13	.03	.04	.04	.04	.03	.06	.04	NS
Agg. TV	138	.03	.03	.03	.04	.03	.03	.03	.02	—*
p of diff.		<.004	NS							NS

PRIVATE SCHOOLS

| | N | Overall Medians | Week-by-Week Medians | | | | | | | Linear Trends |
			1	2	3	4	5	6	7	
Control	159	.03	.02	.03	.01	.03	.03	.02	.03	NS
Agg. TV	167	.03	.01	.01	.01	.02	.01	.02	.02	+**
p of diff.		NS	<.03							NS

Table B-4. Verbal Aggression Toward Authority

BOYS' HOMES

	N	Overall Medians	Week-by-Week Medians							Linear Trends
			1	2	3	4	5	6	7	
Control	135	1.32	.97	.95	.92	.50	.67	1.20	1.60	+ *
Agg. TV	138	.82	.67	.85	.77	.47	.36	.62	.35	− **
p of diff.		< .008	NS							< .002

PRIVATE SCHOOLS

	N	Overall Medians	Week-by-Week Medians							Linear Trends
			1	2	3	4	5	6	7	
Control	159	.39	.14	.10	.09	.17	.18	.19	.27	NS
Agg. TV	167	.36	.13	.07	.18	.33	.17	.16	.08	NS
p of diff.		NS	NS							NS

Table B-5. PHYSICAL AGGRESSION TOWARD AUTHORITY AS A FUNCTION OF EXPERIMENTAL TREATMENT AND INITIAL PERSONALITY DIFFERENCES

BOYS' HOMES

Personality Traits	Cont. Overall Median	N	Agg. TV Overall Median	N	p of diff.
High Agg Anx.	.12	(81)	.03	(81)	NS
Low Agg. Anx.	.26	(52)	.10	(54)	.02
High Neur. Un-Cont.	.16	(64)	.04	(65)	.004
Low Neur. Un-Cont.	.12	(69)	.08	(70)	NS
High Overt Host.	.17	(54)	.04	(60)	.002
Low Overt Host.	.12	(79)	.08	(75)	NS
High Covert Host.	.15	(66)	.04	(55)	.01
Low Covert Host.	.13	(67)	.07	(80)	NS
High Fant. Agg.	.13	(56)	.07	(54)	NS
Low Fant. Agg.	.14	(69)	.05	(75)	.02
High Peer Agg. Nom.	.24	(35)	.07	(40)	.02
Low Peer Agg. Nom.	.07	(32)	.03	(10)	NS

PRIVATE SCHOOLS

Personality Traits	Cont. Overall Median	N	Agg. TV Overall Median	N	p of diff.
High Agg Anx.	.04	(68)	.05	(64)	NS
Low Agg. Anx.	.02	(82)	.03	(87)	NS
High Neur. Un-Cont.	.04	(64)	.04	(74)	NS
Low Neur. Un-Cont.	.02	(86)	.03	(77)	NS
High Overt Host.	.02	(82)	.02	(72)	NS
Low Overt Host.	.06	(68)	.05	(79)	NS
High Covert Host.	.03	(66)	.04	(71)	NS
Low Covert Host.	.03	(84)	.03	(80)	NS
High Fant. Agg.	.02	(53)	.03	(58)	NS
Low Fant. Agg.	.03	(65)	.07	(51)	NS
High Peer Agg. Nom.	.07	(61)	.05	(77)	NS
Low Peer Agg. Nom.	.02	(91)	.02	(80)	NS

Table B-6. VERBAL AGGRESSION TOWARD AUTHORITY AS A
FUNCTION OF EXPERIMENTAL TREATMENT AND
INITIAL PERSONALITY DIFFERENCES

BOYS' HOMES

Personality Traits	Cont. Overall Median	N	Agg. TV Overall Median	N	p of diff.
High Agg Anx.	.91	(81)	.70	(81)	.10
Low Agg. Anx.	1.86	(52)	1.18	(54)	.10
High Neur. Un-Cont.	1.46	(64)	.72	(65)	.004
Low Neur. Un-Cont.	1.15	(69)	.88	(70)	NS
High Overt Host.	1.65	(54)	.76	(60)	.004
Low Overt Host.	1.00	(79)	.83	(75)	NS
High Covert Host.	1.44	(66)	.71	(55)	.04
Low Covert Host.	1.11	(67)	.83	(80)	NS
High Fant. Agg.	1.24	(56)	.90	(54)	NS
Low Fant. Agg.	1.42	(69)	.67	(75)	.002
High Peer Agg. Nom.	1.36	(35)	.93	(40)	.08
Low Peer Agg. Nom.	1.00	(32)	.88	(10)	NS

PRIVATE SCHOOLS

Personality Traits	Cont. Overall Median	N	Agg. TV Overall Median	N	p of diff.
High Agg. Anx.	.34	(68)	.36	(64)	NS
Low Agg. Anx.	.52	(82)	.53	(87)	NS
High Neur. Un-Cont.	.49	(64)	.58	(74)	NS
Low Neur. Un-Cont.	.38	(86)	.26	(77)	NS
High Overt Host.	.48	(82)	.56	(72)	NS
Low Overt Host.	.42	(68)	.31	(79)	NS
High Covert Host.	.42	(66)	.56	(71)	NS
Low Covert Host.	.52	(84)	.31	(80)	NS
High Fant. Agg.	.33	(53)	.56	(58)	NS
Low Fant. Agg.	.72	(65)	.62	(51)	NS
High Peer Agg. Nom.	.57	(61)	.63	(77)	NS
Low Peer Agg. Nom.	.24	(91)	.18	(80)	NS

C

Note on Supplementary Materials

The following additional documentary information, "Supplementary Forms, Analyses and Tables," is available from the authors upon reimbursement for cost of reproduction:

1. Psychological inventory (overt hostility, covert hostility, aggression, anxiety, neurotic undercontrol).
2. Aggressive activity preference measure.
3. Situation test.

4. Aggressive value measure.
5. Viewing habits index.
6. Peer nomination measure.
7. Program rating form.
8. Case history measure.
9. Factor scales derived from the behavior ratings.
10. Factor analysis of peer aggression and authority aggression behavior ratings including factor loadings.
11. Peer aggression scores in the aggressive TV and control conditions, using individual raters as the unit of comparison.
12. Frequency of aggressive and other behaviors toward authority by individual items.
13. Analyses with initial differences controlled.
14. Physical and verbal aggression toward peers and authority as a function of grade level.
15. Physical and verbal aggression toward peers as a function of experimental treatment and initial personality differences.
16. Changes in average aggressive values by institution.
17. Changes in aggressive choices on situations test by institution.
18. Changes in aggressive activity preferences by institution.
19. Changes in recommended sentence by institution.
20. Changes in recommended sentence in boys high in covert hostility and in boys low in fantasy aggression.
21. Changes in the peer aggression nomination measure by institution.
22. Changes in intensity of aggression in fantasy by institution.
23. Changes in physical aggression themes in fantasy.
24. Means and analysis of variance of change in fantasy aggression in boys initially below the median in fantasy aggression.
25. Changes by institution in like-dislike ratings of aggressive shows listed in pre- and post-measures.
26. Changes by institution in like-dislike ratings of nonaggressive shows listed in pre- and post-measures.
27. Physical and verbal aggression toward peers and authority as a joint function of fantasy aggression and overt hostility.
28. Physical and verbal aggression toward peers and authority as a

joint function of fantasy aggression and peer aggression nomination.

29. Characteristics of boys in the experimental and control groups taking the pre-measures only and both pre- and post-measures.
30. Comparison schools and participating institution means on initial personality measures.

References

ALBERT, R. "The role of mass media and the effect of aggressive film content upon children's aggressive responses and identification choices." *Genetic Psychology Monographs,* 1957, *55,* 221–285.

BACHRACH, A. S. *Psychological Research: An Introduction.* New York: Random House, 1962.

BAILYN, L. "Mass media and children: A study of exposure, habits, and cognitive effects." *Psychological Monographs,* 1959, *73,* (471).

BANDURA, A., AND HUSTON, A. "Identification as a process of incidental learning." *Journal of Abnormal and Social Psychology,* 1961, *63,* 311–318.

BANDURA, A., ROSS, D., AND ROSS, S. "Transmission of aggression through imitation of aggressive models." *Journal of Abnormal and Social Psychology,* 1961, *63,* 575–582.

BANDURA, A., ROSS, D., AND ROSS, S. "Imitation of film-mediated aggres-

175

sive models." *Journal of Abnormal and Social Psychology*, 1963(a), *66*, 3–11.

BANDURA, A., ROSS, D., AND ROSS, S. "Vicarious reinforcement and imitative learning." *Journal of Abnormal and Social Psychology*, 1963(b), *67*, 601–607.

BANDURA, A., AND WALTERS, R. H. *Social Learning and Personality Development.* New York: Holt, Rinehart, and Winston, 1963.

BENDIG, A. W. "Factor-analytic scales of covert and overt hostility." *Journal of Consulting Psychology*, 1962, *26*, 200.

BERKOWITZ, L. *Aggression: A Social Psychological Analysis.* New York: McGraw-Hill, 1962.

BERKOWITZ, L. "Aggressive cues in aggressive behavior and hostility catharsis." *Psychological Review*, 1964, *71*, 104–122.

BERKOWITZ, L., AND BUCK, R. W. "Impulsive aggression: reactivity to aggressiveness under emotional arousal." *Journal of Personality*, 1967, *35*, 415–424.

BERKOWITZ, L., CORWIN, R., AND HEIRONIMUS, M. "Film violence and subsequent aggressive tendencies." *Public Opinion Quarterly*, 1963, *27*, 217–229.

BERKOWITZ, L., AND HOLMES, D. S. "A further investigation of hostility generalization to disliked objects." *Journal of Personality*, 1960, *28*, 427–442.

BERKOWITZ, L., AND RAWLINGS, E. "Effects of film violence on inhibitions against subsequent aggression." *Journal of Abnormal and Social Psychology*, 1963, *66*, 405–412.

BRENNER, C. *An Elementary Textbook of Psychoanalysis.* New York: International Universities Press, 1955.

COWAN, P., AND WALTERS, R. H. "Studies of reinforcement of aggression: I. effects of scheduling." *Child Development*, 1963, *34*, 543–551.

EMERY, F. E. "Psychological effects of the western film: a study in television viewing: II. the experimental study." *Human Relations*, 1959, *12*, 215–232.

EPSTEIN, S. "Comments on Dr. Bandura's paper." In M. R. Jones (Ed.), *Nebraska Symposium on Motivation.* Lincoln, Nebraska: University of Nebraska Press, 1962, 269–272.

ERON, L. "Relationship of TV viewing habits and aggressive behavior in children." *Journal of Abnormal and Social Psychology*, 1963, *67*, 193–196.

FENICHEL, O. *The Psychoanalytic Theory of Neurosis.* New York: Norton, 1945.

FESHBACH, S. "The drive reducing function of fantasy behavior." *Journal of Abnormal and Social Psychology,* 1955, *50,* 3–11.

FESHBACH, S. "The stimulating versus cathartic effects of vicarious aggressive activity." *Journal of Abnormal and Social Psychology,* 1961, *63,* 381–385.

FESHBACH, S. "The function of aggression and the regulation of aggressive drive." *Psychological Review,* 1964, *71,* 257–272.

FESHBACH, S. "Aggression." In P. H. Mussen (Ed.), *Carmichael's Manual of Child Psychology* (3rd Ed.), Vol. 2. New York: Wiley, 1970. Pp. 159–250.

FRAIBERG, S. *The Magic Years.* New York: Scribner, 1959.

FREUD, A. *The Ego and the Mechanisms of Defense.* London: Hogarth, 1937.

FREUD, S. *Collected Papers.* London: Hogarth Press, 1925.

FREUD, S. *Beyond the Pleasure Principle.* New York: Boni and Liveright, 1927.

FREUD, S. *Civilization and Its Discontents* (2nd Ed.) London: Hogarth Press, 1957. Originally published in 1930.

FREUD, S. "Creative writers and daydreaming." In *The Standard Edition of the Complete Psychological Works of Sigmund Freud.* Vol. 9. London: Hogarth, 1962(a).

FREUD, S. "Formulations on the two principles of mental functioning." *The Standard Edition of the Complete Psychological Works of Sigmund Freud.* Vol. 9. London: Hogarth, 1962(b).

HARTLEY, E. R. "The impact of viewing aggression: Studies and problems of extrapolation." In *A Review and Evaluation of Recent Studies on the Impact of Violence.* Office of Social Research, CBS, Inc., 1964.

HARTMANN, D. P. "Influence of symbolically modeled instrumental aggression and pain cues on aggressive behavior." *Journal of Personality and Social Psychology,* 1969, *11,* 280–288.

HIMMELWEIT, H. T. *Television and the Child.* London: Oxford University Press, 1958.

HOFFMAN, L. W., AND LIPPITT, H. R. "The measurement of family life variables." In P. H. Mussen (Ed.), *Handbook of Research Methods in Child Development.* New York: Wiley, 1960.

HUMPHREY, R. *Stream of Consciousness in the Modern Novel.* Berkeley: University of California Press, 1958.

KESSLER, J. W. *Psychopathology of Childhood*. Englewood Cliffs, New Jersey: Prentice-Hall, 1966.

LESSER, G. "Application of Guttman's scaling method to aggressive fantasy in children." *Educational and Psychological Measurement*, 1958, *18*, 543–551.

LORENZ, K. *On Aggression*. New York: Harcourt, Brace, and Jovanovich, 1966.

LOVAAS, O. "Effect of exposure to symbolic aggression on aggressive behavior." *Child Development*, 1961(a), *32*, 37–44.

LOVAAS, O. "Interaction between verbal and nonverbal behavior." *Child Development*, 1961(b), *32*, 329–336.

MACCOBY, E. E. "Sex differences in intellectual functioning." In E. E. Maccoby (Ed.), *The Development of Sex differences*. Stanford University Press: Stanford, California, 1966.

MACCOBY, E. E., LEVIN, H., AND SELYA, B. M. "The effects of emotional arousal on the retention of aggressive and nonaggressive movie content." *American Psychologist*, 1955, *10*, 359.

MACCOBY, E. E., LEVIN, H., AND SELYA, B. M. "The effects of emotional arousal on the retention of film content: A failure to replicate." *Journal of Abnormal and Social Psychology*, 1956, *53*, 373–374.

MACCOBY, E. E., AND WILSON, W. C. "Identification and observational learning from films." *Journal of Abnormal and Social Psychology*, 1957, *55*, 76–87.

MC CLELLAND, D. C., ATKINSON, J. W., CLARK, R. A., AND LOWELL, E. L. *The Achievement Motive*. New York: Appleton, 1953.

MELTZOFF, J., SINGER, J. L., AND KORCHIN, S. D. "Motor inhibition and Rorschach movement responses: a test of sensory-tonic theory." *Journal of Personality*, 1953, *21*, 400–410.

MOWRER, O. H. *Learning Theory and Behavior*. New York: Wiley, 1960.

MURRAY, H. A. *Explorations in Personality*. New York: Oxford University Press, 1938.

MURSTEIN, B. (Ed.), *Handbook of Projective Techniques*. New York: Basic Books, 1965.

MUSSEN, P. H., AND RUTHERFORD, E. "Effects of aggressive cartoons in children's aggressive play." *Journal of Abnormal and Social Psychology*, 1961, *62*, 461–464.

NUNBERG, H. *Principles of Psychoanalysis*. New York: International University Press, 1955.

PETRINOVITCH, L. "Psychobiological mechanisms in language development." In G. Newton and A. D. Riesen (Eds.), *Advances in Psychology*. New York: Wiley, 1970.

PIAGET, J. *The Language and Thought of the Child*. New York: Meridian Books, 1955.

PREMACK, D. "Reinforcement theory." In D. Levine (Ed.), *Nebraska Symposium on Motivation*. Lincoln, Nebraska: University of Nebraska Press, 1965, 123–180.

RILEY, M. W., AND RILEY, J. W., JR. "A sociological approach to communication research." *Public Opinion Quarterly*, 1951, *15*, 444–460.

SALTZ, G., AND EPSTEIN, S. "Thematic hostility and guilt responses as related to self-reported hostility, guilt and conflict." *Journal of Abnormal and Social Psychology*, 1963, *67*(5), 469–479.

SCHRAMM, W., LYLE, J., AND PARKER, E. B. *Television in the Lives of Our Children*. Toronto: University of Toronto Press, 1961.

SCOTT, W. A., AND WERTHEIMER, M. *Introduction to Psychological Research*. New York: Wiley, 1962.

SEARS, R. R., AND OTHERS. "Some childrearing antecedents of aggression and dependency in young children." *Genetic Psychology Monographs*, 1953, *47*, 135–234.

SEARS, R. R. "Relation of early socialization experiences to aggression in middle childhood." *Journal of Abnormal and Social Psychology*, 1961, *63*, 466–492.

SEEMAN, W. "The Freudian theory of daydreams: an operational analysis." *Psychological Bulletin*, 1951, *48*, 369–382.

SIEGEL, A. E. "Film-mediated fantasy aggression and strength of aggressive drive." *Child Development*, 1956, *27*, 355–378.

SINGER, J. L. "The experience type: some behavioral correlates and theoretical implications." In M. R. Ricker-Ovsiankina (Ed.), *Rorschach Psychology*. New York: Wiley, 1960.

SINGER, J. L. *Daydreaming: An Introduction to the Experimental Study of Inner Experience*. New York: Random House, 1966.

SINGER, R., AND SINGER, ANNE. *Psychological Development in Children*. Philadelphia: Saunders, 1969.

WALTERS, R., AND E. THOMAS. "Enhancement of punitiveness by visual and audio-visual displays." *Canadian Journal of Psychology*, 1963, *17*, 244–255.

WALTERS, R. H., THOMAS, E. L., AND ACKERS, C. W. "Enhancement of punitive behavior by audio-visual displays." *Science*, 1962, *136*, 872–873.

WERTHAM, F. C. *Seduction of the Innocent*. New York: Rinehart, 1954.

WILLEMS, E. P., AND RAUSCH, H. *Naturalistic Viewpoints in Psychological Research*. Holt, Rinehart, and Winston, 1969.

ZUBIN, J., ERON, C. D., AND SCHUMER, F. *An Experimental Approach to Projective Techniques*. New York: Wiley, 1965.

Index

181

149, 152–153, 155–157; physical, 63, 72, 77, 81–82, 108, 155; physical, in fantasy, 98, 107–109, 117; prosocial, 105, 117; provoked, 69, 72, 96; punishment of, 8, 36, 61, 77, 93–94, 96, 135, 138, 143; reduction of by nonaggressive fantasies, 15–16; reinforcing aspects of, 17, 33; sex differences in, 26–50; shaping of, 16–17; and socioeconomic class, 32; toward authorities, 68, 69, 72–74, 77, 82–83, 86, 93–94, 96–97, 99–101, 120, 126–130, 133, 141, 142, 144, 146, 148, 156; toward peers, 66, 68–69, 72–74, 77–80, 82, 83, 85, 91, 93, 94, 96–97, 99–101, 104, 107, 111–112, 118, 120, 126–130, 133, 138, 141, 146, 148, 156; unprovoked, 69, 72; values of, 47, 64, 95, 112, 130, 135, 141, 146, 148; verbal, 63, 72, 77, 81, 83, 93, 120; vicarious, 90, 122, 153–156

Aggressive attitudes, 46, 95–112

Aggressive behavior, 1, 4, 8, 25–28, 31, 33, 34, 36, 38, 40, 42, 43, 46–48, 56, 66–94, 102, 105–108, 112–116, 123–124, 130, 139–141, 145–146, 148, 157–158

Anger, 22, 23, 39, 65, 125, 133, 156; experimental manipulation of, 39–40, 43

Attitudes: aggressive, 46, 95–97, 141; measures of, 56, 64, 66, 95, 97, 105, 125, 130; paper and pencil tests of, 40, 56; toward television diet, see Television diet, attitude toward

B

BANDURA, A., 13, 23, 36–37, 43
BERKOWITZ, L., 15, 40–41, 42
Boys' homes. See Institutions

Buss-Durkee Inventory of Aggression, 40, 60

C

California Personality Inventory, 60

Catharsis hypothesis, 39–40, 47–48, 119, 149, 152, 155–157

Censorship and control of violence on television, 45

Child rearing, 29, 159

Clinical studies, 28, 31

Cognition, differentiation of, 9, 25, 154–155

Cognitive controls, 153–155

Cognitive development and effects of fantasy, 43, 154

Cognitive support, 152–156

Comedies, effects of, 150

Conditioning, 8, 10, 14, 21; of fantasy, 14

Conflict, measurement of, 60, 90, 125, 130, 135

Conformity, 13

Control in experimental research, 27–29

Correlational methods, 28–29, 33

Culture: and punishment of aggression toward authorities, 94; and reinforcement of aggression toward peers, 94

D

Daydreams, 3, 5, 7, 14, 153

Death, 2, 45

Delay of gratification, 11

Delinquency, 26–27, 31; and reaction to film violence, 40; and television viewing habits, 32–42

Deprivation: of dreams, 154; of fantasy aggression, 154

Developmental psychology, 39, 159

Dreams, 3, 7, 152, 154

E

Ego control of aggression, 91, 142, 156

Emotional disturbance and television viewing habits, 32–33, 42

Index

Values: measures of aggressive, 64,
    66, 95–97, 101–102, 108–109,
    112, 124, 130, 135, 138, 141,
    146, 148
Violence, 4, 10; censorship of, on
    television, 45; effects of, on
    television, 11–15, 17–19, 25,
    30, 33–34, 44–45, 48, 90, 141,
    144, 149, 153, 155, 156–158;

objections to, on television,
    18–19

W

WALTERS, R. H., 13, 21, 23, 36–37,
    41, 43
WELLES, O., 2
Word association tests, 39